*Disability in Mission* does a wonderful job of helping the church see people with disability as a mission force rather than a mercy project. Drawing from biblical examples of how God uses human weakness to display divine strength, the authors provide compelling stories of those who, in their weakness, have become strong in Christ. This book is a true gift to the church, as it challenges us to reorient how we see our brothers and sisters with disability and instills kingdom dreams to those who may otherwise think they cannot contribute to the Great Commission.

**Michael Y Oh**
**Global Executive Director / CEO, Lausanne Movement**

This book contains a vital message that needs to be heard and heeded, not just in cross-cultural mission agencies, but by the whole Christian community. Its message certainly contains a powerful challenge, but it is above all an inspiring encouragement. What an amazing God we worship, who became weak for us in Christ and wants to use us—not in spite of our weaknesses but through them!

**Vaughan Roberts**
**Rector of St Ebbes, Oxford**

I grew up as the son of medical missionaries in Nigeria. I remember many missionaries struggling, but I don't remember missionaries with disabilities or with children with disabilities. This important book explores the power of missionaries with disabilities, or with children in their families whose faith and call enables others to see both their gifts and struggles. For people in lands where missionaries have often been associated with dominant Western cultures, these missionaries enhance a sense of mutuality that is built on both gifts and limitations. The witness of their work and call also embodies the proclamation of an authentic gospel in which power and powerlessness are very different in God's eyes. It also entails a church that affirms the dignity and the gifts of all of God's people. We are all called to be the church together.

**Bill Gaventa**
**Director, Summer Institute on Theology and Disability**

The call in the last decade has been to recast the life and mission of the church. We no longer think of mission as being *to* people with disabilities but *with* them. *Disability in Mission* shows us what this looks like in reality. Here we find firsthand accounts of people with disabilities engaging in the *missio Dei* to and from the ends of the earth. We able-bodied persons can now reimagine the church as one body with many members. The diversity of gifts and tongues will sound again as they sounded at Pentecost.

**Amos Yong**
**Director, Center for Missiological Research**
**Professor of Theology and Mission**
**Fuller Theological Seminary**

We can never be too weak for God, but we can be too strong for him. We can never be too simple, but we can be too clever; never too poor, but we can be too rich. This book boldly and biblically takes us to the great virtues of weakness and brokenness, which in our folly we would cover and hide. It takes a long time for many of us to discover our weakness is our strength. That, after all, is where God is most at home!

**Charles Price**
**Senior Pastor, The Peoples Church, Toronto, Canada**

*Disability in Mission: The Church's Hidden Treasure* is a gem of a resource—one that I will recommend again and again! This groundbreaking volume begins with insightful and practical theology that lays a solid foundation for the compelling and diverse stories it contains. Written by people touched by disability who have served Christ and his kingdom around the world, the personal testimonies serve as illuminating examples of how God loves to display his power in weakness, for his glory. This book will challenge your mind, move your heart and motivate you to encourage people with disabilities to go forth as essential participants in the mission of God worldwide.

**Stephanie O Hubach**
**Research Fellow in Disability Ministries, Covenant Theological Seminary**
**Author of *Same Lake, Different Boat: Coming Alongside People Touched by Disability***

David Deuel and Nathan John take an important step forward in mission studies—they highlight how people with disabilities have participated in God's ongoing redemptive mission in the world. By building on a strong biblical foundation and offering concrete examples of various people with different disabilities participating in the mission of the church, the authors demonstrate that when it comes to being witnesses, no one is disabled. *Disability in Mission* contributes to a growing conversation that calls congregations to shift from imagining ministry to people with disabilities to embracing and supporting ministry by people with disabilities.

**Benjamin T Conner**
**Professor of Practical Theology**
**Director of the Graduate Certificate in Disability and Ministry**
**Western Theological Seminary**

*Disability in Mission* represents a paradigm shift for the medical community! It challenges all of us who practice medicine and global health to go beyond healing . . . and to understand that people with disability have an important role to play in ministry. And even in overseas missions. Every medic with an interest in mission should read this book.

**Peter Saunders**
**CEO, International Christian Medical and Dental Association**

*Disability in Mission: The Church's Hidden Treasure* is a gem of a resource that goes a long way towards reminding us that mission is incomplete without the active involvement of those from the margins. Those thought to be 'weak' are indispensable in mission, as is evidenced by the fact that God's mission began at the margins. Reading this book takes you through a journey of how persons with disabilities and their families transformed the landscape in which they served by sharing their gifts with these communities and as a result enriched God's kingdom.

**Anjeline Okola, Programme Coordinator**
**World Council of Churches, Ecumenical Disability Advocates Network**

God's economy is predictably the inverse of ours. The disciples considered Mary's 'waste' of costly perfume to be worthy of rebuke. Jesus countered by declaring that her act of worship would reverberate throughout history. The world around us speaks the language of power. The gospel travels on radio waves of human frailty.

One of the most effective missionaries I have ever known contracted polio in her childhood. It didn't stop Elinor from pursuing her missionary call. God took her to a primitive tribal group in the rugged mountains of New Guinea. There she learned the language, strapped a chair to two poles, and was carried from village to village by an honor guard of strong warriors. They gave Elinor the name 'Bad Legs.' She shared God's love, proclaimed the gospel and eventually helped to translate the New Testament into the tribal language. 'Bad Legs' became the adored queen of those isolated mountain valleys. She was God's 'chosen instrument' for a very special task.

I've personally known some of the people mentioned in these pages, and witnessed the supernatural impact of their humble service. May God help us to recognize, appreciate and facilitate the priceless contribution of these 'gifted ones' for his greater glory.

**Steve Richardson**
**President, Pioneers USA**

*Disability in Mission* should move and inspire churches and missionary organizations to rethink the role of the disabled in the mission field. Professor John and Dr Deuel offer a vision of lives affected by disability making a real difference, while disqualifying the stereotypical views on disability. The authors make their case that the disabled and the mission field are a perfect match—a match literally made in heaven.

**John Nugent**
**President and COO**
**Joni & Friends**

What does it really mean that when we are weak, Christ is strong? This volume presses that paradox home through remarkable stories of God's grace in translating disability into gospel power in a variety of missionary contexts. Read this and be challenged to deepen your engagement with and commitment to disability and mission.

**Wei-Han Kuan**
**State Director, Church Mission Society Victoria**

Wow! What an amazing book. What moving stories of disability serving God's mission! When we hear the word 'disabled,' we tend to think 'dis-abled,' but this is not true in human life, in Christian life and ministry, or in Christian mission. In a world that worships a particular version of physical perfection and attractiveness, this book shows how God turns things upside down . . . or rather, the right way up! An invaluable rethink of the essential role of disability and weakness in God's mission to the world.

**Peter Adam, Vicar Emeritus, St Jude's Carlton**
**Former Principal, Ridley College**
**Melbourne, Australia**

An army that refuses to recruit, train and use its best soldiers would be considered foolish and ineffective. Yet many churches and mission boards do exactly that, refusing to even consider that an adult or family experiencing disability could be effective in proclaiming the gospel in a cross-cultural context. God clearly states that the so-called weaker member is indispensable to the church, and the contributors to this book make compelling biblical and experiential cases for the unusual missionary effectiveness of those the world denigrates because of disability. May this book open the eyes of mission boards, pastors, senders and missionaries to God's power and purposes in considering those experiencing disability for the mission field.

**John P Knight Sr**
**Director of Donor Partnerships, Desiring God**

Dr Deuel and Professor John have given the kingdom a great gift in *Disability in Mission*. Since Paul and his (apparent) visual disability launched out on the first mission trips, missions and disability have walked—or rolled!—the same path. Deuel and John show how God's great design uses disability to fulfill his Great Commission. By gathering perspectives on how disability and mission buttress one another, Deuel and John have made this rich trove of kingdom thought accessible to all believers.

**Cameron Doolittle**
**Founding President and CEO, Jill's House**
**Washington, DC**

This wonderful collection of stories is an important contribution to understanding how all of us, able and differently abled, can participate in God's mission. For centuries we have operated from a model of mission and power: money, people, strategy, speed and scale. Our society reinforces this model with its messages of success, performance and stardom. Those who are more dependant and vulnerable are frequently seen as a problem to be solved. This book beautifully draws us back to the central gospel message of God's grace and life flowing from what we consider to be weakness. We desperately need to grasp hold of the counter-cultural message of this book for mission and for the whole of life.

**Paul Bendor-Samuel**
**Executive Director, Oxford Centre for Mission Studies**
**Director, Regnum Books**

This book stunned me speechless. I read here the very objections I faced, and which God led me past when I began and continued my own career in mission. The stories in *Disability in Mission* reveal that disability can be God's secret servant for greatest usefulness in his kingdom—a truth central to my story, too. Read these stories, be blessed, and have your world changed.

As a child, I suffered polio that left me profoundly disabled. But I knew God wanted me to be a missionary someday. My parents encouraged me, but my church didn't. One mission agency said no, but World Team said they would take the chance, accepting me to do Bible translation for the Kimyal tribe from the rugged mountain ranges of West Papua. A Kimyal man recently said, 'Praise God. The people . . . happily carried the missionary named Elinor Young as she needed to go from church to church to teach the children. . . . I must do as she did and carry the gospel of Christ to all.'

Read this unique book! Let its stories and truth inspire you, disabled or not, to carry the gospel of Christ to all.

**Elinor Young**
**Former World Team Missionary to Papua**

These stories of some of God's mightiest missionaries are potent testimonies of his power made perfect in human weakness and imperfection. These families and individuals with disabilities are God's secret pearls, crafted to conform to the image of Christ through the adversities of disabilities to display his finest and most beautiful workmanship while advancing his kingdom. Their presence and voices in the mission field inspire suffering people to embrace and experience the truth of 'Christ in us, the hope of glory.'

**Stephanie Chung, Chair and Associate Professor**
**Special Education Department, Cairn University**

**Walter Chung, Director and Professor**
**Online Counseling Psychology Programs, Eastern University**

# Disability in Mission

## *The Church's Hidden Treasure*

Lausanne Library

FOREWORD BY JONI EARECKSON TADA

# Disability in Mission

*The Church's Hidden Treasure*

EDITED BY

DAVID C DEUEL AND
NATHAN G JOHN

**Disability in Mission: The Church's Hidden Treasure**

Hendrickson Publishers Marketing, LLC
P. O. Box 3473
Peabody, Massachusetts 01961-3473
www.hendrickson.com

ISBN 978-1-68307-201-0



This book was compiled in collaboration with Joni and Friends (see page 170).



*Printed in the United States of America*

*Second Printing — September 2019*

Cover design by John Ruffin

**Library of Congress Cataloging-in-Publication Data**

Names: Deuel, David C., editor.
Title: Disability in mission : the church's hidden treasure / edited by David C. Deuel and Nathan G. John ; foreword by Joni Eareckson Tada.
Description: Peabody, MA : Hendrickson Publishers, 2019. | Includes bibliographical references.
Identifiers: LCCN 2019009422 | ISBN 9781683072010 (alk. paper)
Subjects: LCSH: Church work with people with disabilities. | People with disabilities--Religious life. | Missions. | Evangelistic work.
Classification: LCC BV4460 .D5724 2019 | DDC 259/.44--dc23
LC record available at https://lccn.loc.gov/2019009422

For Elena Down, who showed by her life how God works powerfully in mission through disability.

(1972–2017)

Elena had agreed to contribute to this book, but she died unexpectedly from a pulmonary embolism on a flight to Geneva in March 2017. We dedicate this book to her memory.

Elena completed a law degree in 1997 and immediately wanted to apply her skills in missions. Despite being profoundly hearing-impaired, she did not want to be identified as 'disabled,' and resisted invitations at first to minister amongst the deaf just because she herself was deaf. However, over time she came to see her deafness as a gift to minister to the deaf.

She worked as a volunteer at the Nambikkai Project for the Deaf in rural India. She learned the local sign language and taught the young women to swim (in their saris!). Elena wrote in her diary: 'I learned a lot in India—about myself, my values and God's values. I could see that my deafness was something that could open doors to enable other people to know God.'

Returning to Australia, she worked as a lawyer with the Australian Government Solicitor in Melbourne and then Canberra.

For eight years Elena served at the Attorney-General's Department, in copyright law, international law, human rights policy and disability discrimination. This included playing a key role as principal legal officer in Australia's negotiations on—and subsequent signature of—the UN Conventions on the Rights of Persons with Disabilities. Elena was chosen as a torch-bearer in the Sydney Olympics torch relay, carrying it for two legs in Canberra.

From 2003 to 2004 she took two years' leave without pay to work with the deaf in China. During this time, she mastered both written and spoken Mandarin—'an impossibility for the deaf'—and acquired several different Chinese sign languages. She established a support program for parents of deaf children and mentored deaf university students. She saw needs which others hadn't seen, and tackled them with imagination. For example, she recruited a group of deaf adults to tutor parents of deaf children in sign language. She also acted as a catalyst in forming a church for the deaf.

This book is the poorer without Elena's chapter, but her legacy lives on to eternity in many lives.

# Contents

# Chapter Summaries

**Chapters 1 and 2**: These look at passages from Scripture that help us appreciate how weakness, vulnerability and disability embody the gospel, and have power to bring transformation. They describe how weakness is central to the redemptive plan of our all-powerful God, and how disability often, although not always, results in an experience of weakness. Drawing on Paul's story and then on Moses' story, David Deuel describes how weakness is the means of success, not failure, for when Christians are weak, then they are strong. God, who resists the proud and gives grace to the humble, often confounds earthly powers through the weakness of his chosen vessels. It is through weakness that the mission of God is advanced.

**Chapter 3**: Bonnie Armistead describes how the birth of Anna, with Down syndrome, caused them to doubt God's calling. Their story shows that Anna's disability is actually an inseparable part of their calling. They witness God's sovereign purposes in the way he shapes them, redirects their ministry and impacts the community in which they work.

**Chapter 4**: J M Paul describes a deep joy from sharing in the life and mission of their son's few years on earth. Through Adam's profound disability and their own struggles, they experienced a King who was able to work through broken people to restore broken things. Adam's disability profoundly shaped their family and their approach to mission. Adam taught them that this is God's mission, and we play a humble, often broken, role in that mission. In a moving tribute, J M describes how Adam's legacy will live on in their mission journey and in the journey of many others whom God challenged and changed through Adam. She concludes 'In the days God ordained, he has worked beyond our imagination in Adam's life and, in painful but beautiful ways, he continues to work through his death. We know that this is not the end of the story.'

**Chapter 5**: Barry Funnell relates how an accident and resultant paraplegia transformed his selfish independence and pride into complete dependence on God. Barry's life-threatening accident also gave him a sense of urgency as he realised 'all human beings are only one last breath away from eternity.'

Rather than being a stumbling block to missions, his disability has served as a springboard. God used him to make great strides in Bible translation through ten years in Malawi, five years in Tanzania and various consultancies throughout South East Asia.

**Chapter 6**: This outlines a beautiful story from the early twentieth century where God works powerfully in weakness through the ministry of Paul Kasonga, who is disabled with leprosy, and Olive Doke. For Paul and Olive, weakness was the very basis of their service to each other, to Christ and to the nation of Zambia. David Deuel outlines how Kasonga and Doke's work was formative in a movement that saw upwards of 80 percent of the Zambian national population turn to Christ, and continues even today through its spiritual descendants.

**Chapter 7**: Paul Lindoewood shows that when properly cared for and resourced, a lifelong wheelchair user with limited dexterity and communication impairments can be involved in mission! Between 1996 and 2005 Paul and his wife Rachel worked as mission partners with the Methodist Church in Kenya, based in Maua Hospital, around five hours northeast of Nairobi. Paul describes a mind-set of exclusion within many churches and sending agencies. He challenges them to look beyond the disability and to play a role in enabling those with disability to participate in mission.

**Chapter 8**: What of disability and short-term mission teams? Jeff McNair draws on his experience on a short-term mission trip which included five people with disability. He describes how their presence changed many aspects of the trip in positive ways. It impacted the team members themselves, in addition to those being served through the activities. Jeff provides some useful pointers for future efforts in including people with disability in short-term teams.

**Chapter 9**: This brings an example of God working through weakness in mission, largely from a home-based setting. Natalie Flickner's multiple disabilities have given her empathy and a knowledge base to become a strong and powerful advocate for children with disabilities. She describes how God has called her, in all her inadequacy, and equipped her through her disability to develop materials to help missions respond to children with disability. Her ministry is very different from what she had imagined she was called to. Yet, with a humble awareness of God's faithfulness in the past, she explains that she can look forward with anticipation to how God will continue to use her.

**Chapter 10**: Justin Reimer provides thoughtful guidance in making the decision as to whether to go overseas. He describes the process of preparing the family to live in Ukraine, and preparing their sending church and the receiving field to accommodate his son with disability. Life in a foreign country is hard enough, and there are added challenges when that culture degrades those with disability. But God supplies grace and intimacy that is greater than any obstacle we may face. The Reimers' desire is to see the glorious gospel of Jesus Christ proclaimed by his people *to* those with disabilities and proclaimed *by* those with disabilities.

**Chapter 11**: Now we explore how the member care movement can help promote a supportive and caring approach in seeking to enable people with disability to serve. There are considered risks here for mission agencies and churches. Only when these risks are taken will our mission workforce be complete. Deanna Richey explains that we are beginning to see churches and missions increasingly valuing the role of people with disability. She provides a framework for agencies, and more specifically for those involved in member care, to consider how best to support and send them.

**Conclusion**: Finally, we draw out the common themes to encourage churches, mission agencies and potential missionaries to consider how disability might be used by God in missions.

# Foreword

In 1989, I was asked to address the participants of Lausanne II, the International Congress on World Evangelization in Manila. The subject of my message centred on the church's responsibility to give the gospel to 'the poor, the crippled, the lame, and the blind,' and I was excited with the prospects of awakening the Lausanne gathering to Jesus' mandate in Luke 14. I knew instinctively that the need was greatest among churches and people with disabilities in countries like the Philippines. Back then, I had travelled to only a handful of less-developed nations. The needs in the Philippines focused my mind. I had never seen so many maimed and injured people dragging themselves along the dirty sidewalks, wearing flip-flops on their hands. I managed to make friends with many of them living in makeshift lean-tos between our hotel and the conference centre.

Most were paraplegics, some were blind, and a few were amputees. But none of these dear people had ever seen anyone like me. When I extended a greeting to them, gesturing awkwardly with my limp hand, they seemed hesitant to touch me. They stared wide-eyed, few of them having ever seen a quadriplegic who had no use of legs *or* arms. When I spoke to them about my love for Jesus, they seemed fascinated. I could almost read the thoughts behind their amazed expressions: *How can this lady trust God the way she is?!*

The same thing happened at the Manila Pastors' Conference, an additional Lausanne convocation for several hundred Filipino Christian leaders. I shared with them the same Luke 14 message. Observing my obvious limitations, they seemed especially curious about my faith in Christ. During lunch break in the main hall, many watched my husband Ken feed me a hamburger. Again, I felt curious eyes examining us, and I could almost read their thoughts: *How wonderful that God has made her so happy amidst such a difficult disability! How does she do it?*

I was experiencing firsthand the power behind 2 Corinthians 4:7,10, 'But we have this treasure in jars of clay to show that this all-surpassing power is from God and not from us. . . . We always carry around in our body the death of Jesus, so that the life of Jesus may also be revealed in our body.' The more obvious the weakness in the messenger, the more beautifully adorned is the gospel he shares! People with disabilities are the burning bushes spoken of in Exodus 3—we cause curious onlookers, even skeptical ones, to turn aside and 'see this strange sight—why the bush does not burn up' (Exodus 3:3). People with disabilities, especially missionaries with disabilities, make others hungry for the Bread of Life, and thirsty for the Living Water. They provoke the question *Is God truly powerful enough to sustain his joy in a quadriplegic? I must find out more!*

This shows exactly why people who '*seem* to be weaker are indispensable' in the body of Christ as together we strive to make Jesus known to an unbelieving world (1 Corinthians 12:22, italics added). To the natural eye, people with disabilities *seem* to be weaker; they *seem* to be the least likely candidates for kingdom work. But to the spiritual eye—to those who value what God values—people with disabilities add depth, richness, and a platform for explosive power in kingdom advancement.

To quote the editors of the book:

> Herein lies the problem with the mission movement. We are inclined to assess our performance according to the standards of the secular world. This success-oriented approach can cause us to squeeze our potential missionaries into rigid molds in which they have to be intelligent, strong, agile, and have high energy: the Type A personality. This can mean that the mission movement selects only missionaries who have certain personality types, or alternatively it can tend to squeeze people who are different shapes into the same mold. When applying the world's standards of success we therefore discount people who are different, who can't be squashed into an ableist mold. Almost by definition, people with disability will not fit into an ableist mold, and nor should they. The stories you will read in the following pages are of missionaries who do not fit that mold.

The book you hold in your hands is vitally important to the church and its mission movement. Its stories of people with impairments are the proof-text for 2 Corinthians 4:7–12. They are modern-day validations of the need for Christian workers on the field whose disabilities adorn the gospel. I appeal to leaders in agencies and denominations to consider what I believe to be a compelling case for selecting and training qualified people with disabilities for mission work. It is an idea whose time is long overdue—especially considering that our preeminent example is the apostle Paul himself!

So, enjoy the stories, consider the arguments, study the Scriptures and start asking questions. Ask how you can enlist, and even exploit, people's limitations for the glory of God on the mission field. Do you lead a mission agency, a denomination or a church? Are you a wheelchair-user seeking to hold out the gospel in places where most say, 'You can't go there'? This book is your guide to taking next steps in inviting God's all-surpassing power to explode through your mission or church outreach! Turn the next page, and let the adventure begin.

Joni Eareckson Tada
Lausanne Board Member
CEO, Joni and Friends International Disability Center

INTRODUCTION

# The Church's Treasure: People with Disability on Mission

Nathan G John
Australia

## The Disabled Mission Movement

'Disability ministry is not disability ministry
unless the disabled are ministering.'[1]
Joni Eareckson Tada

Not many have heard of Kaputula Kasonga, whose story is outlined in Chapter 6. The fact that 80 percent of Zambians consider themselves evangelical Christians is in large part due to this man's work. Now, I wonder what mental image you might have of him. Perhaps you imagine a tall, imposing figure with the voice of Martin Luther King Jr. In fact, he was a weak man with a disability. From his youth, Kasonga had multiple severe and worsening disabilities that came with leprosy, including difficulty in walking, chronic pain, inability to write and recurrent illnesses. Nevertheless, he was a man whom God wanted to use for his glory. His story provides an excellent example of how God has chosen to work through the foolish and weak things of the world to show his glory.

Kasonga's story is not an isolated example. There are many such stories. Such a pattern makes no sense to a world that is obsessed with outward beauty, intelligence, power, strength and popularity. Yet our God often works in ways that are at odds with the world's values. Cheryl Stinchcomb outlines this vividly in her poem-prayer, 'The Upside-Down Kingdom.'

**"The Upside-Down Kingdom"**
**by Cheryl Stinchcomb**

The world says: Blessed are the strong and powerful, for they can get what they want.

Jesus says: Blessed are the weak, for my power is made perfect in weakness. (2 Corinthians 12:9–10)

The world says: Blessed are you when people speak highly of you, for everyone will know of your good reputation.

Jesus says: Blessed are you when you are insulted, misunderstood and persecuted, for great will be your reward in heaven. (Matthew 5:11–12)

The world says: Blessed are the knowledgeable and educated, for they will go far in this life.

Jesus says: Blessed are those who qualify in kingdom wisdom, for God has chosen the foolish things of the world to shame the wise. (1 Corinthians 1:27–29; 1 Corinthians 2:6–16)

The world says: Blessed are you when life is easy and you have everything you need, for that is where happiness is to be found.

Jesus says: Blessed are you when you suffer, for suffering produces perseverance; perseverance, character; and character, hope. (Romans 5:3–4; 2 Corinthians 4:16–18)

The world says: Blessed are those who live a good life, for God will use them.

Jesus says: Blessed are those who have messed up and know his grace, for he who has been forgiven much, loves much. (1 Timothy 1:15–16; Luke 7:44–48)

The world says: Blessed are the healthy and strong, for they can win races and achieve success.

Jesus says: Blessed are the feeble and weak-kneed, for God has chosen them to show his all-surpassing power and glory. (2 Corinthians 4:1–12)

Lord, we live in a world that craves power and riches, forgive us when we conform more to the ways of this world and help us to choose your path of humility and weakness. (Philippians 2:1–11; Matthew 20:28)

Lord, we live in a world that sees only the visible and judges on the outside, forgive us when we see only with our physical eyes and help us to see the invisible work of your kingdom around us. (2 Corinthians 4:18)

> Lord, we live in a world that is temporary and will wither and die, forgive us when we are so engrained in this world that we live as if this is all there is; help us to invest in your kingdom that will last forever. (Matthew 6:19–21; 1 Peter 1:17–19)
>
> Lord, you have made us to be in the world, but not of it. Thank you for sending Jesus to show us how to live here in this world. Give us eyes to see this world as you see it and to live here and now as citizens of your upside-down Kingdom.
>
> Amen.

Approaches to mission have sometimes reflected a secular business model that values strength and power. That is to say, we have sometimes replaced the words of God with the traditions of human beings (Matthew 15:3). Our hope is that this book will help to turn the mission movement upside down, so that it more closely reflects an upside-down kingdom.

At the time of the 2016 Paralympic Games there was a trailer entitled 'We are the Super Humans' and through it the constantly repeated line 'Yes I can.' It showed the amazing feats of those with disability, and promoted a 'we can' attitude. You can find it online. One rugby player in a wheelchair crashes at high speed into another; despite disabilities people climb mountains and play in bands. In many ways, they are super humans! These Paralympians have overcome so much to be able to achieve so much. Still, physically they can rarely compete with their non-disabled counterparts. And if we use the same criteria for measuring success—speed, strength and skill—then a person with disability will usually be second best.

Herein lies the problem with the mission movement. We are inclined to assess our performance according to the standards of the secular world. This success-oriented approach can cause us to squeeze our potential missionaries into rigid molds in which they have to be intelligent, strong, agile, and have high energy: the Type A personality. This can mean that the mission movement selects only missionaries who have certain personality types, or alternatively it can tend to squeeze people who are different shapes into the same mold. When applying the world's standards of success we therefore discount people who are different, who can't be squashed into an ableist mold. Almost by definition, people with disability will not fit into an ableist mold, and nor should they. The stories you will read in the following pages are of missionaries who do not fit that mold.

This idea of an upside-down kingdom is not only radical for the secular world but may well cause mainstream mission agencies to cringe. The likes of Kasonga would perhaps not have passed the first step in the standard recruitment process. It would be considered 'too dangerous' to have someone so 'vulnerable' and 'weak' on the field.

Our aim in our missional endeavour is surely for people to know Christ as their Saviour, to have a real and personal relationship with God, a dependence on him, and interdependence within the body of believers. Perhaps ideally suited to this role are missionaries who, due to their disability, are completely dependent on God, humble in their leadership and dependent on others in their churches.

The selection process my wife and I went through did not aim to solicit the strengths in our human weaknesses, and didn't question if our human strengths were actually also our spiritual weaknesses. We were selected on the basis of our human strengths well before our encounter with disability. We had six degrees between us, including a DPhil from Oxford and two professional medical fellowships. We were physically fit, psychologically stable and, of course, well-grounded in our theology. Surely we were well-equipped to serve God, right? Wrong! Our training was incomplete.

We arrived on the field feeling confident to tackle the ministry God had called us to, and then our world fell apart. Our first child was born with a profound disability and our world was turned upside down. Weakness, on many levels, became a permanent resident in our lives. Yet, as we were already mission partners, our mission agencies stuck by us, and although it was not always pretty, we struggled on, serving God. Were we to go before a mission selection committee now, we would probably fail on multiple levels. Our vulnerability, the messiness of our family, and of course having a profoundly disabled daughter would make the agency terribly irresponsible to send us abroad.

Yet, some eight years after this encounter with brokenness, I can look back and say that nearly all the rich fruit we have witnessed has come because of—not in spite of—our brokenness. Most of my spiritual growth and ministry impact have come from my experience of disability, vulnerability and pain. Just one example is the establishment of an India-wide movement for disability inclusion in the church called Engage Disability.[2] Our involvement was inspired by our daughter, Abby, and intimately informed by my experiences of life and church with her. Developing this movement has taken patience, gentleness, a willingness to accept people for who they are, empathy, passion and a heart for disability. All of these are skills that I have developed through my life experience of raising a child with profound disability.

## Hardships Can Prepare People for a Special Purpose

Kasonga's experience, my journey, and that of my co-editor David Deuel all tell a similar story; a story I have heard echoed by so many who are not only broken but are also being used by God in effective ministries and missions. Indeed, many of the case studies in this book outline a similar pattern whereby God has worked powerfully in missions *through* disability, and not just *in spite of* disability. The question should not be, 'How could this be the case?' but, 'Why do we find this so surprising?' Isn't the biblical pattern one where God uses 'foolish' and 'weak' people to achieve his purposes? Yes, there is a biblical precedent for God using the powerless and disabled for his glory. Saul was depressive. Moses was a stutterer. Jacob had his limp. Paul had his thorn. God chose to use these weaknesses for his glory. Perhaps their struggle with weakness actually made them good leaders.

We learn in the Bible that God uses the weak and foolish things to show up the wise and to achieve his purpose; and that the seemingly weaker parts of the body of Christ are actually the indispensable parts.

Perhaps most significantly, let us take note that Jesus chose fishermen, tax collectors and a Samaritan woman to spread his word and turn the world upside down. Nowadays, might some mission selection panels, with their onerous testing and health requirements, have rejected Jesus? Of course he was perfect, but he was a failure by human standards. He had a rag-tag group of followers. He was a man of suffering. He experienced weakness. And eventually he was disfigured on the cross. Yet he turned the values of the world upside down as he defined his kingdom not in physical or professional terms, but by establishing an upside-down kingdom that was far from worldly!

So, have we been sending the wrong mix of people to the mission field? Have we inadvertently selected a whole group of people who have it together, who are bright-shining examples, who are worthy to be followed? Do the mission field and the mission community suffer from a lack of people with disability and vulnerabilities? The body of Christ, and indeed the mission movement, need all the different parts, including those with disability, to play their role in order to function effectively.

Paul makes the radical assertion that those parts of the body that 'seem to be weaker are indispensable' (1 Corinthians 12:22). If we trust the Bible's portrayal of the body and apply that to the church and its mission agencies, then is it too bold to say that the mission movement is itself disabled? The mission movement could be incomplete because we exclude the seemingly weak members from playing their part.

## The Scope of This Book

Our central thesis is that disability-inclusive missions provide major opportunities for ministry in the twenty-first century. This was recently recognised by the Lausanne Movement, which encouraged church and mission leaders 'to think not only of mission among those with a disability, but to recognise, affirm and facilitate the missional calling of believers with disabilities themselves as part of the Body of Christ.'[3]

This thesis is equally relevant for any outreach ministry. There are new and creative approaches to mission that are disability-friendly. As we reflect on cross-cultural mission, we now see people from everywhere going out to everywhere. Indeed, in this globalised world we can undertake cross-cultural mission at our own doorstep. Geographical location is almost irrelevant, and what we learn from missions is applicable for many local ministries.

We define disability quite broadly to cover impairments, activity limitations and participation restrictions from various physical and non-physical causes.[4] This umbrella definition encompasses various weaknesses, emotional issues and vulnerabilities to which this book speaks. Even if not a formal 'disability,' those who are suffering, grieving or experiencing any manner of other difficulties will identify with struggles outlined here, and find a biblical theology of relevance to their own experiences. We cite a body of biblical and popular writings on how God redeems and works through weakness, pain and suffering.

Our specific focus on cross-cultural missions and disability is because:

- First, international mission is typically out of bounds for people with disability. Whilst there is increasing acceptance in a Western context that people with disability can play a unique role in their local church and its ministry, this has generally not been reflected in the worldwide mission movement.
- Second, despite the availability of books outlining the positive impact of people with disability in ministering in their own families and churches, we are not aware of any that explore the role of people with disability in global missions.
- Third, disability has particular relevance in missions, given its high incidence in many of the low and middle income areas where missions is active. Disability is commonly seen as a curse or a punish-

> ment from God, whereas suffering and pain do not always have the same stigma attached. So, disability provides a means of demonstrating the nature and ways of God, beyond the understanding of the cultures in which we work. God is revealed in unique ways in such settings, as he uses the seemingly weak things, the things 'that are not,' to challenge an entire worldview and illustrate the power of the gospel.

The idea of drawing in vulnerable people and people with disability may appear radical, even reckless, to some. We hope that these extreme stories will (1) inspire those with disabilities and vulnerabilities to seek to be involved in ministry; (2) inspire churches and communities around them to facilitate their ministry; and (3) embolden the church to think beyond God working *in spite of* our disability, towards acknowledging that God intends to work powerfully *through* our disability.

This will ultimately require a paradigm shift in the culture of the sending churches, mission agencies and the receiving organizations in the field. Once this is achieved the mission movement will no longer be disabled. It will no longer be missing an indispensable part of the body of Christ.

Let me finish with a story of a brave bishop from the third century who understood a concept that we need to rediscover. During the persecution of the early church, Lawrence, who was a deacon in the church of Rome, was ordered to bring the treasures of the church before the emperor.[5] He collected all the poor, the sick, the lame, the elderly and disabled people he could find, took them to the emperor and said, 'See, here are the treasures of the church!' He made his point, which is our point in this book, that those with disability are treasures in the church. The emperor was not so pleased, and had Lawrence burned to death most cruelly.[6]

CHAPTER 1

# Disability and Biblical Weakness

David C Deuel
Joni and Friends Christian Institute on Disability
United States

Weakness does not neatly equate with disability, but they do often coexist. Furthermore, disability often, although not always, results in an experience of weakness. Weakness is central to the redemptive plan of our all-powerful God. It is the means of *success*, not failure, for when Christians are weak, then they are strong. Strength through weakness might seem paradoxical, but in fact it reveals the glory of God and crushes human pretension. God, who resists the proud and gives grace to the humble, confounds earthly powers and refutes worldly wisdom through the weakness of his chosen vessels. It was through weakness that the forces of evil were defeated and judged; and it is through weakness that the mission of God is advanced today.

As King over all creation, God is carrying out his mission plan for this world through his messengers. To make them successful agents, he commissions and empowers them, but often he must first reduce their strength in order to infuse them with his power. This is biblical weakness. Many of God's messengers experience weakness, sometimes as a result of disability, including Paul, Moses, Gideon, David and those whose stories are told in this book. To a group of beaten-down and weak captives, Isaiah the prophet said, 'He gives power to the weak and strength to the powerless. Even youths will become weak and tired, and young men will fall in exhaustion. But those who trust in the Lord will find new strength' (Isaiah 40:29–31 NLT). This common thread of weakness among God's servants assures us that God will meet our inadequacy with his strength, in whatever task he calls us to accomplish. Moses, Isaiah and Paul were all called by God to deliver his words and perform his works, but Paul perhaps gives us the fullest picture of weakness in the life of God's servants.

The common pattern of God working in weakness is epitomised in Jesus, who was sent to earth in weakness and died on the cross in weakness. He humbled himself, taking on the form of a servant to complete the greatest mission of all time: to bring salvation to a lost and dying world.

God uses weak messengers. It is therefore not surprising that weakness is a common experience in God's mission. Biblical history leaves us a record of responses to disability, both good and disappointing.

## Disability and Weakness in Biblical Times

Misunderstanding about weakness has often led to people with disabilities being stigmatised. In Israel's early days, religious leaders misunderstood God's law, believing that the same law that required God's people to provide for and protect persons with disabilities also prohibited priests with disabling conditions from serving. This error was rooted in the misunderstanding that priests with disabilities who were restricted from offering sacrifices should not serve as priests at all. In short, it assumed that people with disabilities should not undertake leadership roles. This prejudicial mind-set often isolated and alienated them by stigmatising them. This was carried to an even greater extreme later in Israel's history when people with disabling conditions sometimes were not allowed to be present in the synagogue when the Torah was read, or to enter the Qumran community of ancient Israel near the Dead Sea.[1]

Acts of exclusion of the seemingly weak find no place in Jesus' teaching and practice. Jesus' care for people with disabilities shocked the religious establishment, and continued to do so into the period of the early church. Instead of being kept out, some with disabling conditions directly approached Jesus or were brought to him on stretchers. In one case, a man was lowered through a hole cut in a roof. These acts mark the dawning of a new day for the inclusion of people with disabilities in the church. Jesus breaks down barriers of isolation and invites people with disabilities to come to him. He provides them with dignity and sees their true value as treasures created in the image of God for his purposes and glory. So why now do churches and mission boards reject 'weak' people with disabling conditions from serving as pastors, missionaries, and in other forms of leadership?

## Biblical Weakness

Weakness is a loss of strength or ability that affects everyone, and changes through our lives. Disability terminology changes over time, but with each new term one characteristic remains: namely, that some ability is lacking. This negative framing of disability is a reason why the church struggles to understand it and appreciate it. Seeing weakness and strength through a biblical lens brings a different perspective.

The Bible teaches that to be human is to be weak (Genesis 1; Psalm 19; Romans 1) for we are frail, transitory and mortal beings (Romans 5:6; 6:19; 8:26). From Genesis to Revelation, Scripture recognises the weakness of humankind or the 'flesh.'[2] As David Alan Black writes in *Paul, Apostle of Weakness*, 'Weakness is not simply the occasional experience of sickness or powerlessness, but a fundamental mark of the individual's worldly existence.'[3] As Solomon explains in Ecclesiastes, while we may experience temporary strength, to pursue strength is ultimately a chasing after the wind. We all eventually become weak. The apostle Paul taught, in a nutshell, that our 'whole being is dependent upon God and that men and women as creatures of God (like Adam and Eve) are susceptible to the limitations of all creation.'[4]

Owning our weakness can lead to biblical strength, which is rooted in dependence. Because God created the universe, he depends on nothing, but God designed humanity, indeed all creation, to depend on him. In the Fall, mankind sought independence and power, and, sadly, became weaker as sin weakened the creation. Ironically people's unquenchable thirst for independence and power resulted in weakness that would ultimately crush them. In contrast, as is evident from the Bible, when we depend on God we allow him to enable us with his strength. True biblical strength is a consequence of a right and dependent relationship with God. God's plan of redemption is to bring human beings back into perfect dependence upon, and union with, him. Therefore, paradoxically, it is in our weakness (human) that we are strongest (most dependent on God). Similarly, when we are disabled we are perhaps more likely to be dependent on God; to be God-abled.

Ultimately, God in his grace overcame our human weakness, caused by separation from him, by sending his Son in weakness as a babe, to die as an adult in weakness on a cross, at the hands of human power. In Christ, the paradigms of power and weakness were turned upside down. Through this weakness of the cross God restores our relationship with himself, allowing us to depend on Christ dwelling in us, and giving us true biblical strength. The cross nullifies the root cause of weakness by restoring us to relationship with God in astounding ways.

## *Weakness as God's Theatre*

Our weakness shows us our need for God—the creator and sustainer of the universe—to enable us. One of Moses' weaknesses seems to have related to his slow speech and heavy tongue, likely representing a speech difficulty or possibly a speech disability. Yet he was God's weak vessel to display God's might. In our small-minded ways, we might question why it is important to God to use weakness. Our weakness is God's theatre for displaying his strength before a watching world. Even the angels are watching God's theatre of weakness. This explains why God chooses to work through weakness. But why do we need weakness?

First, God uses disability and any resultant weakness as part of our growth. To comprehend this, we must look at weakness from two points of view: our own weakness, and weakness in others. We will understand weakness in others by first understanding it in our own experience. From our self-study, we will learn to share empathy with those who are weak. Then we will be ready to help them from our position of weakness (2 Corinthians 1:3–5).

Second, weakness in others is our opportunity to serve them and to help them grow. Crucially, the apostle Paul says, 'we must help the weak' (Acts 20:35) because Jesus meets the needs of the weak through faithful fellow-believers. Helping others in sincerity before a watching world is a critical part of God's plan for weakness. In this way the weakness of those with disability is in fact a part of their ministry to the world. Their weakness is an opportunity for others to serve God through serving them. This is how those people are bearing witness to Christ.

How does weakness help us and others grow? God uses weakness to create a healthy vulnerability, which then allows spiritual growth. Like the apostle Paul, the prophet Jeremiah came to realise that he suffered at the hands of his enemies because he followed the Lord's leading. Today, we might say with hesitation that the Lord caused his sufferings. But we would be only partially correct, because God allows us to experience weakness for his sake and ours. Jeremiah similarly came to accept God's plan for his weakness through those who devised schemes against him.[5] In short, our weakness is a battle that God will win as his power and purpose are displayed though our vulnerability.

## *Paul Experiences God's Use of Weakness*

Throughout Paul's ministry, God chose to work powerfully through his weakness; this weakness was a celebration of God's triumph through disability and hardship.[6] The triumph of weakness can be won against various forms of resistance, opposition, or inability. These are God's battlefields, where he claims the victory. For the apostle, weakness often came through people who challenge him. But he also experienced weakness in the form of personal suffering, a thorn in the flesh. Opposition from without and fear from within weakened Paul. He was afflicted on every side with conflicts and other forms of opposition, and with fears and weakness within.

Paul's weakness from the outside came from those who opposed him and his ministry. Some opponents had entered the Corinthian church while he was away, and they sought to undermine his ministry. Their chief criticism was that Paul was weak, particularly when he was present! He didn't look like an apostle or teach like one. Paul was just not impressive, using their measure of strength. Interestingly, before Paul met Jesus on the road to Damascus he was known as Saul, a strong man who used his power to persecute those of 'the Way.' But Paul was changed. These opponents were using popular ideas of what a leader should be from Corinthian culture, setting them up as biblical standards. In the face of this opposition, Paul articulated his views about weakness in 2 Corinthians 10–13. Pastors, missionaries and other ministry leaders will relate to the apostle's challenge. Paul wrote to the Corinthians to defend himself against their criticism. The approach that he took in the letter is a beautiful picture of accepting criticism and then turning it on its head with biblical teaching. Rather than denying weakness, Paul argued that he was most certainly weak, and that weakness is ideal for an apostle, indeed for anyone in Christ's church. The weaker the better!

Weakness from the inside was Paul's thorn in his flesh. The thorn was likely some sort of infirmity as suggested by the idea of an object causing pain, and of 'flesh' in its most literal sense, body. This was the most common meaning of the term 'weakness' in Paul's world. The imagery is probably more precisely a stake in Paul's flesh, large and very painful! That the stake was some form of physical obstruction to Paul's ministry seems clear. It may also have formed one of the points of accusation. The fact that he sought the Lord in prayer three times to remove the thorn, but was not cured, may remind us of our own suffering. Those of us who have a disability or some other form of suffering find comfort in the fact that even the apostle Paul, who healed others in his ministry, could not heal himself. Nor would God heal him, although he could have.

Paul described his weakness as a messenger of Satan, but God sovereignly used the messenger for his own purposes, just as he did with Job. Paul did not state the relationship between the messenger and the thorn. In fact, the apostle carefully used the passive construction, 'there was given to me,' to avoid identifying a sender. But who gave it? We can surmise that Paul did not identify a sender because it is not easy to explain responsibility when it comes to describing God's and Satan's roles in physical infirmities. This was true with Job too.

Whether the thorn was from God or Satan, clearly God intended to use it. Paul saw God's purposes in his weakness, particularly when he made statements like 'for Christ's sake, I delight in weaknesses' (2 Corinthians 12:10). Weakness is God's design, not bad luck or random chance. Paul gave three reasons for his thorn, all of which may apply to us as children of weakness in this world. It served: (1) to cut off his flow of pride for receiving the revelations; (2) to position him in need, so that he could receive Christ's help; and (3) to help him see the power of Christ's working in him that he might otherwise miss.

These three things were not in Satan's best interest. Paul's spiritual weakness, that is, his propensity toward pride in receiving the revelations that give him apostolic standing, was tempered by his physical weakness. This leads us to conclude that our weakness causes us to depend upon God and not on ourselves. We cannot appreciate God's strength and his glorious purposes unless we first experience our own weakness. What can we draw from this?

When the church lays hands on someone, commissioning them to perform its work, this special blessing affirms and celebrates a call and giftedness in that person. Sadly, people with disabling conditions have usually been last in line to experience such affirmation and celebration. Sometimes, they are excluded from being in line, either by local church leadership or by mission agencies. Imagine what it would mean for a young girl or boy in a wheelchair, or someone who is hearing- or sight-impaired, to realise that they too can take part in the church's mission if they are called and gifted.

What the casual reader might miss is that Paul described his conflict as all-out spiritual war.[7] The opposition to him had moved beyond persecution to a full-scale attack. He was 'harassed at every turn—conflicts on the outside, fears within' (2 Corinthians 7:5). What is crucial is that the apostle treated the internal and external opposition as one. Paul's opponents—Satan being the chief—had power that they used against him and the mission that he was trying to conduct. But God's matchless power overrode the opposition in both the attacks and Paul's physical diminishment.

## *The Sphere of Christ*

It is in the 'seeming weakness of the world' that the foolishness of the world is confounded by God's wisdom. People are not called because of their wisdom, their talents, or their status and stature. God calls out of his strength and provision (1 Corinthians 1:26).

God explained his ways to Paul in these clear words, 'My grace is sufficient for you, for my power is made perfect in weakness' (2 Corinthians 12:9). The imperfect strength of this world cannot compare with what God offered Paul. And beyond human comprehension, weakness perfects God's strength.[8] No wonder Paul could say with conviction, 'for when I am weak, then I am strong' (2 Corinthians 12:10). Yes, it is as easy as that. Let us remind ourselves that Paul's transparent look at himself and his own weakness was done in the context of his mission to the Corinthian church, which was probably the church that brought him his greatest challenge. Weakness of all sorts is most prevalent where the battle for new converts and new local churches is hottest. For those of us who love the Lord's mission, this comes as welcome encouragement.

It is beautiful to think of Paul's weakness operating in the sphere of Christ (2 Corinthians 10:13–15). To understand this, we must picture the distinction between heaven and earth. Having prepared the way for us through his death on the cross, Jesus waits for us in the heavenly places. In our earthly realm, characterised by worldliness, believers are subject to all forms of weakness. We feel pain, experience disability, suffer spiritual confusion and meet all of the darkness of the world's chaos. But as believers in Christ, we already have access to the heavenly places, the sphere of Christ, and this world's darkness begins to lift. The stench dissipates. In Christ, Paul ascends to the heavenly places (Ephesians 1:3,20). And the apostle invites those of us who are weak to join him. The sphere of Christ offers unlimited power, comfort and peace.

## *What Characterises Paul's Weakness?*

Paul describes weakness more precisely and thoroughly in 2 Corinthians 10–13 than anywhere else in Scripture. Although he does not intend to present his Corinthian readers with a complete theology of weakness, he offers us enough detail to understand it, and what it accomplishes for him and his opponents.

- *What is weakness like in Paul?* Paul shows that although weakness is humble and gentle (2 Corinthians 10:1), it can be bold (10:1–5), confident (10:7), and can have authority (10:8). It manifests itself consistently whether he is physically present or writing from a distance. Weakness is unimpressive (10:10), but is not inferior (10:15).

- *What does weakness do for Paul?* Weakness does not allow Paul to compare himself with others (10:12); does not boast in accomplishments (10:13–15); elevates others (11:7–9); does not judge by appearance (10:7); brings glory to God (11:30); and gains strength from the cross of Christ (12:9).

- *What does weakness do to Paul's opposition?* Powerfully, it demolishes strongholds, arguments and pretension (10:4), and shames the strong and the proud (1 Corinthians 1:25–27). David Black summarises:

  > If being weak means acting like a father instead of like a ruler, speaking with simple instead of proud words, preaching the gospel free of charge instead of demanding apostolic wages, humbling oneself instead of boasting in oneself, leading the churches by example instead of forcing one's will upon them, then Paul is happier to admit, 'I *am* weak.'[9]

Weakness transforms Paul. No wonder he uses the analogy of the human body to teach the value of weakness in the church (1 Corinthians 12:22–23):

> Even the least attractive and most inconspicuous members of the church are important and should be treated with respect. The weaker members not only have a proper place in the church, but are in fact 'much rather necessary,' for all the members of the body are interdependent and interrelated. Therefore, because they are actually indispensable, Paul says they only 'seem to be' (*dokounta . . . hyparchein*) weaker and unnecessary.[10]

In short, 'God not only places the necessary weaker members in the body, but also gives more honour to them (1 Corinthians 12:24).'[11]

## *Paul's Exposé of Weakness*

People with disabilities can bring a dependency that the church lacks and desperately needs. Too often our churches condone, or even adopt, the dominant societal narrative, with independence or autonomy as our ultimate goal. Yet, our earthly journey is a classroom to learn dependency upon the Lord. Paul wrote this exposé to give us a clearer picture of how dependency worked out in his own life, and therefore, how it might work out in ours. His conclusion? Our weakness displays our vulnerable humanity and thus our need to rely upon God. This allows God to work in and through us to achieve his mission.[12] This leads to the inevitable conclusion that 'there are many people in ministry too strong to be useful. There are no people in ministry too weak to be useful.'[13]

Ultimately, then, weakness transforms lives. What does it mean for us to be weak? It means that we must become weary and wait for God's strength. It means that we must suffer before he can heal us. It means that we must fail so that our Lord can succeed for us. It means that we must lose so that he can win. It means that we must die weak so that he can give us new and perfect life. How we need weakness!

## Conclusion

By God's design, he chose Moses, Isaiah and Paul in weakness and disability, then sent them on their missions. Was this mission sabotage? By no means. God used their weakness to disable pride, dismantle opposition and display his power to a watching world.

If the church's mission needs weakness, the church needs to allow people with disabilities to express their call and giftedness for the glory of Christ. They will demonstrate the value of weakness, as well as the need for weakness. Shouldn't we pray for a greater presence of disability and weakness in the church? Let's include those whom St Lawrence saw as the church's treasure in the church's mission.

CHAPTER 2

# Moses, Messenger of Weakness

David C Deuel
Joni and Friends Christian Institute on Disability
United States

We too often expect that weakness leads to failure and strength to success. In God's missions, he inverts this paradigm, turning weakness into success and strength into failure. God's enabling is the pivot, which he himself sets in motion. Humility, dependency and faithfulness in the face of disability and suffering beat all human odds. God, using the full resources of his creation, always completes his mission. Exodus 3–15 chronicles Moses' journey from weakness to enablement, as God turns creation upside down to make Moses' mission successful.

God often uses people to accomplish his plans. Christ-followers are his agents in this world, sometimes referred to in Scripture as his 'messengers.' In power, God's messengers deliver his words and perform his works. Joseph and Moses stand tall as Israel's first two national messengers. They conduct back-to-back missions as God works out his plan of redemption. Joseph's mission takes him from Israel to Egypt; Moses' mission from Egypt back to the Promised Land. Israel, an entire nation, goes with them. In worshipful reflection, the psalmist praises God for sending both leaders to his people, for this is how the Lord remembers his covenant. 'Remembering' means planning, and then taking action to provide for and protect his people. Think of how this worked out when God sent Joseph ahead into Egypt. Years later, God would use Joseph to rescue his people from a devastating famine in Israel. Similarly, the Lord sent Moses to rescue his people from Egyptian persecution.

## God Sets Up the Exodus

Through the cruelty and deception of Joseph's brothers, God deploys Joseph to Egypt to make him a leader of the great Egyptian empire in advance of a devastating famine. When crops begin to fail, Joseph blesses the Egyptians with his God-given wisdom, preserving them and his own people from starving. On the day that Joseph's brothers finally come before him to beg his forgiveness for selling him as a slave into Egypt, Joseph tells them, 'It was not you who sent me here, but God' (Genesis 45:8). And later, 'You intended to harm me, but God intended it for good' (Genesis 50:20). The good that God intended was Israel's preservation during a time of regional famine. God's plan included his growing a small clan of families into a large and powerful nation. God's missions typically accomplish many aspects of his plan all at once.

Israel's exodus and its annual celebration, the Passover, are foundational in Scripture. The celebration of Passover is taken up in every historic period, and practically every book of Scripture. Later biblical writers look back to it in each generation, even into the New Testament, when Jesus' contemporaries freely identify him as a second Moses. These events and the subsequent giving of God's law formed Israel's foundation as a nation. That makes Moses' story special. Moses stands out as the most extraordinary human leader in the Old Testament. No one surpasses him. The book of Deuteronomy closes with this reflection on his life:

> Since then, no prophet has risen in Israel like Moses, whom the Lord knew face to face, who did all those signs and wonders the Lord sent him to do in Egypt—to Pharaoh and to all his officials and to his whole land. For no one has ever shown the mighty power or performed the awesome deeds that Moses did in the sight of all Israel.
>
> (Deuteronomy 34:10–12)

Conspicuously absent from this glowing reflection on Moses' leadership is any mention of his power of speech. Moses performs the mighty acts of God, the magnificent signs and wonders of his day; but he only speaks to God, to Aaron and to a few others that we know of. Leaders of Moses' magnitude normally make moving and impressive speeches, public proclamations and royal edicts. Why is nothing said about Moses' spoken messages?

Moses' life is a story of weakness, demonstrated by his slowness of speech and tongue. Whether this was a specific disability has been contested by theologians and somewhat depends on one's definition of disability. Using a functional and inclusive definition (see introduction) his issue seemingly has many characteristics of a disability leading him to avoid speaking in public. For the purposes of this chapter we refer to this limitation as a disability.

Moses initially declined God's commission, using this speech disability as an excuse. Yet, God reminds Moses that he both gave him his disability and chose him to be his messenger to Egypt. That is why Moses' mission in weakness might seem paradoxical until we grasp that weakness is the occasion for God's enablement. In the end, Moses led the exodus from Egypt, the crowning event in the Old Testament, with a disability; a true messenger of weakness.

## *Moses Declines God's Commission*

The wisest teachers in Pharaoh's court trained Moses to rule as an Egyptian leader, perhaps even as a Pharaoh. In contrast, God chose to teach Moses to shepherd his people in the ignobility of the wilderness. Moses' zeal for God's people and his humility before the Lord were essential character qualifications. But crucially, it was God himself who selected and trained Moses. There was no screening process with multiple candidates. Moses was destined in the eternal plan of God to lead the mission. God makes no mistakes. Moses' disability was no mistake.

One day, Moses was tending his sheep near Mount Sinai, the very place where God would later give him the law. As Moses led his sheep into new pastures to graze, the Lord's angel appeared to him in a burning bush and began speaking to him. After instructing Moses about God's holiness, the angel commissioned the prophet to go as a messenger to Pharaoh, the Egyptians and to God's people. As God's agent, Moses must perform God's mighty acts of judgment in Egypt. But the humble shepherd, weak in speech, must also *speak* God's messages. Moses panicked.

Courageously, Moses *was* willing to perform the plagues against the Egyptian slave masters and was not afraid to die for the mission. But because of his speech problem, he questioned his ability to complete God's mission, and declined his assignment. It is unclear exactly why speech was Moses' weakness. Commentators speculate about the cause. But one thing is certain: God responds as if Moses' inability is a dis-ability. How do we know this?

When God responds to Moses' refusal, his answer is striking: 'Who gave human beings their mouths? Who makes them deaf or mute? Who gives them sight or makes them blind? Is it not I, the Lord?' (Exodus 4:11). The words deaf, mute, sighted and blind all indicate physical disabilities.[1] The four terms play a crucial role in interpreting the passage. Moses is not *afraid* to speak; he just doesn't think he *can*.

Moses' reasons for not delivering God's messages might sound straightforward, but Moses subtly crafts his response to blame God for his disability.

## *God Enables Moses*

God's response in Exodus 4:11 doesn't just shed light on Moses' disability; it also reveals something about God's relationship to disability. Wouldn't we expect God to say, 'Who makes those unable to speak, able to speak?' God has a fuller understanding of Moses' limitations than Moses does. This verse addresses God as the one who assigns disabilities, and sets the stage for his helping people with disabilities through *his* people. In Moses' case the helper will be Aaron. Yes, God teaches his servant that he is the God of ability! God will provide for Moses; Moses only needs to trust and obey.

God is not just the cause of disability, but the upholder, enabler and final rescuer of people with disabilities. To see God as responsible is very different from blaming God for disability, which would be a serious error. The prophets echo God's role: 'In that day, declares the LORD, I will assemble the lame and gather those who have been driven away and those whom I have afflicted' (Micah 4:6 ESV). This again reminds us that God assumes sovereign responsibility for those with disability; and it brings assurance that he will one day heal them. As the psalmist proclaims, 'The LORD gives sight to the blind . . . ' (Psalm 146:8).

In the book of 2 Samuel we read of Jonathan's son Mephibosheth, who had a physical disability and felt alone and abandoned. Not only did he lose his entire family, but he was unable to provide for himself in a world that relied on physical labour to survive. In faithfulness, God used King David to provide for him. David also protected him from enemies who wanted to kill him for misdeeds that his grandfather Saul committed. Not only did God provide for and protect him, but Mephibosheth sat at the royal table with David's family. David even assigned managers to care for Mephibosheth's fields so that he could enjoy the dignity of human labour and success. And so we see again how God meets the needs of people with disabling conditions through others. Fittingly here, God chose a king to care for an orphan with a disabling condition.

If God calls us to serve in his mission, he will enable us. And if he gives us a mission assignment, he also empowers us for the task. For those who have a disability, as 80 percent of us will as we age, this passage brings reassurance. Disability should not keep us from experiencing the joy of serving God. What is more, our greatest joy in serving God may come from helping others with their disabilities, as David and Job did. Might we say with Job, 'I was eyes to the blind and feet to the lame' (Job 29:15). Perhaps Jobs have been the hand of God to many people with disabling conditions throughout history.

Why would the God of all power create Moses with a disability and commission him, rather than heal his disability? Wouldn't that have been easier than wrangling with him about how he could do what God asked him to?

## *God Holds Up the Arms of Moses*

When God responded to Moses' refusal, he explained his role in helping those with disability. In short, the Lord challenged Moses to look beyond his speech limitations to the ways God enabled him, even through others. God said, 'I will help you speak and will teach you what to say' (Exodus 4:12). Moses would then 'put words in his [brother Aaron's] mouth' (4:15). Amazingly, this was how Israel would hear the voice of God for a period of over forty years. What God limits in each of us he provides through other people.

How far will God go? He will unleash all of creation! God also sent his angel, his own mysterious presence, to accompany Moses on every step. It was the angel who assisted Moses in performing the plagues against Pharaoh and the gods of Egypt. The angel gave Moses the power to engage all of God's creation against those who oppressed and mistreated God's people. One by one, the plagues pummeled the Egyptian enemies who had murdered Israelite infant boys and beaten the Jews into building Egypt's infrastructure. All creation bowed before the Lord. The angel, who commissioned Moses at the burning bush, never left his side until the mission of leading the people to the Promised Land was complete. Like Moses, who could not enter the land flowing with milk and honey, the angel stopped on the plains of Moab before the people entered their land.

Finally, we would miss an important detail in the Moses story if we did not ask whose plan it was for Aaron to be Moses' spokesman. God proposed the solution, not Moses. Moses had refused God's mission because no workable solution was obvious, but God's answer was that Aaron be the mouth of Moses for the voice of God. Through difficult conversations with God, Moses agreed to receive God's messages. But God still needed Moses to conduct one final mission—to compose and sing his praises and lead others in songs of praise.

### *Moses Praises God in Song*

God put songs in Moses' heart despite his speech disability. In two passages of Scripture, we are told that the prophet composed and sang praises to God in worship. That's right. Moses could sing before others, but not speak to them. Moses' compositions, the Song of the Sea and the Song of Moses, are two of the finest lyric poems in Scripture. So while he found it impossible to speak to people, he ministered to them beautifully and courageously in the words of the songs he wrote. Moses recited the following song 'from beginning to end in the hearing of the whole assembly of Israel' (Deuteronomy 31:30).

> Listen, you heavens, and I will speak;
>   hear, you earth, the words of my mouth.
> Let my teaching fall like rain
>   and my words descend like dew,
> like showers on new grass,
>   like abundant rain on tender plants.
> I will proclaim the name of the Lord.
>   Oh, praise the greatness of our God!
> He is the Rock, his works are perfect,
>   and all his ways are just.
> A faithful God who does no wrong,
>   upright and just is he. (Deuteronomy 32:1–4)

It's interesting that Moses used the terms 'speak,' 'words of my mouth,' and 'proclaim.' It's as if he was saying 'Look at me! God has given me a voice to speak!'

## Conclusion

It is striking that the man closest to God was the least able to communicate his experience to others.[2] Moses' disability did not prevent God from using him. This is weakness pressed into service. Significantly, God (to whom Moses had no trouble speaking) never offered to cure Moses' speech disability. But Moses could capture the beautiful connection between praise and poetic art. He had a disability; he also had a gift.

God performed mighty acts through Moses' disability. In time, and through suffering, Moses eventually became the servant God called him to be. This reluctant messenger gave Israel God's perfect law and also built the first earthly tabernacle, so that God could dwell among his people. It was through Moses that God spoke Israel's official statement of faith: 'I forgive wickedness, rebellion, and sin' (see Exodus 34:7). To this day, God's people remember Moses as God's prophet, teacher and national leader. As God enabled his hesitant messenger, God will enable us too—very often in and through our suffering, disabilities and weaknesses.

God can perform mighty acts through our disabilities. Paradoxically, in weakness, we can ask God to enable us with his unlimited power and wisdom. Our weakness magnifies God's greatness.

CHAPTER 3

# Kingdom Impact through Weakness and Disability

Bonnie Baker Armistead
Java, Indonesia

## Down Syndrome—Our Divine Appointment

'Whether you turn to the right or to the left, your ears will hear a voice behind you, saying, "This is the way; walk in it."'
(Isaiah 30:21)

The call came at night. The results of the amniocentesis confirmed a 99.99 percent chance that the child I was carrying, our second, would have Down syndrome. My husband and I, each holding a phone to our ear, looked into each other's eyes as we tried to process the information the doctor had just given us. Down syndrome—what did that mean? I had never known anyone with Down syndrome before, and in the panic of that moment I assumed the worst. After all, why else had there been such a push for prenatal screening throughout the pregnancy? But there was no more time to continue processing: the doctor was speaking again. 'I need to know what you want to do.' We were still too stunned to understand what the doctor was saying. Ten seconds, twenty seconds of silence went by. And then my brain finally made sense of the doctor's words, their meaning finally registering—seven months into the pregnancy, we were being given the option to abort because of the evidence of genetic defect. Very quietly, very gently, a knife had been placed into our hands.

Something was going to die that night: either it would be the baby girl that I was carrying, or it would be our dream of serving as overseas Christian workers. In that moment of decision, the years of preparation for mission work flashed before my mind's eye: four years of seminary training for both of us; five years serving among an unreached people group. How could we have so missed hearing the Lord's call that he would now pull us off the field like this? Was abortion perhaps an option in our case? And then my brain registered another voice speaking, but it was not the doctor's voice. This voice spoke to my spirit, my brain making full sense of the words: *Honour him, and he will honour you*. Though I didn't know if this was a verse from Scripture, I knew in my spirit beyond any doubt that there was only one choice that could come anywhere near to honouring the God of all life, and that choice was life. So, very quietly but very firmly I found my voice and handed the 'knife' back to the doctor: 'Abortion is not an option for us,' I said. 'We take as the Lord gives.' In saying this, I knew that I had spoken life to our baby girl in honour of the living God. At the same time, those words spoke death to our dream (and what I thought was our call) to serve as overseas missionaries.

## *The Forging of a Biblical Worldview*

News about the diagnosis of Down syndrome spread quickly among the leadership of our main sending church in Baltimore. We were on a regularly scheduled furlough and planned to return to Indonesia three weeks after the baby was born. We now had some quick rethinking to do. The doctor had put me on bed rest for what had become an increasingly high-risk pregnancy, so we went to our mission pastor and let him know we thought it best that we stop our furlough circuit. Immediately, our church's arms went around us. Within the week, the mission pastor had extended the contract on the house the church had made available for another year. All expectations for public speaking and meetings with mission supporters were suspended. Besides doctors' visits, I was allowed two trips out of the house a week, one for my mid-week women's Bible study and the second for the Sunday church service. Otherwise, I was to be on bed rest.

Our church, in very concrete ways, became a haven of stability for us as we braced ourselves to receive this very unknown addition to our family. Meals were sent daily from the church's kitchen ministry. The former missions pastor, who had recruited my husband to be part of the church's mission outreach in Indonesia, met with him regularly for personal mentoring. Two months before our baby was due, my husband and I entered into a time of listening and waiting, wondering what our future would hold. Our supporting churches joined us as we listened and waited, our future suspended until we knew what we were dealing with. As we entered into this season of doldrums, we all assumed that with a cognitively disabled child on the way, the Armisteads would not be returning to Indonesia. However, no one had heard conclusively from the Lord to this end, and so we watched, we waited and we prayed . . .

### *Fortifying a Weak Theology of Suffering*

Meanwhile, during this time of sudden quiet, I began to ask God the hard questions that could no longer be suppressed. The first was more an accusation than a question: *How could you do this to us?!* But I quickly moved on to quoting Scripture. *According to your word in Psalm 23:6,* YOU PROMISED *that 'goodness and love will follow me all the days of my life.' How is this good?!* Doubt that God was true to his word began to whisper. Could this God of the Bible be trusted? God wasn't feeling so safe to me at that moment.

Though I was unaware of it, my personal theology at the time was that if, to the best of my ability, I did everything 'right,' (that is, in line with what I perceived was God's will), then God would protect me from 'bad' things happening as evidence of his approval. So here we were, serving among an unreached people group at the uttermost ends of the earth in line with Jesus' commission in Acts 1:8. Indeed, if we went any farther, we would start to come back around the other side of the globe. How could we not be in line with the Lord's will? What's more, before leaving for Indonesia, I'd spent four years getting my MDiv after I'd become a Christian in college through the ministries of InterVarsity Christian Fellowship. When it came to choices about what I was going to do with my life, I had consistently chosen to act for God and his kingdom. That's how I made it to seminary and how I met and sensed God leading me to marry my husband, Brent Armistead. 'Mr Indonesia' is what my husband was called at seminary, because he knew exactly where he was going after graduation. Now, our circumstances conflicted with my theology, and the conflict was rising to the surface. This 'crisis' led to some pretty hard feelings towards God. Like Job, I felt betrayed. What had we done to deserve this?

Thankfully, unlike with Job, God was not silent during this time of confusion. In the quiet of my living room where I sat perched every day on a borrowed sofa, facing an empty wing chair, I perceived the Lord speaking to my challenge from Psalm 23:6. *Goodness? How do you see it, Bonnie? What is your definition?* Now, that was a good question, but after some pondering, I realized that I was pretty blank when it came to a definition of goodness. However, I certainly knew what it was not! 'Sinking our ship' was not good! Plunging us into an unknown future was not good! My suffering, both physical and emotional, was not good!

But then, as I heard myself talking, reason kicked in. *Hey, wait a minute . . . If nothing good can come out of suffering, then Jesus would never have come into this world. Didn't God pull off one of the greatest feats of goodness that human history has ever known in the giving of his Son, who suffered, bled and died for us so that humanity could be reconciled to God? Didn't Jesus embrace the unknown when he embraced Death? In the face of* that *unknown, he trusted God, that God would restore his future to him. And by the way, who's the captain of the ship, anyway? If Jesus is the captain, isn't it his prerogative to steer the ship where he wants to go?* Other questions bubbled up. *But surely, if God were pleased with this ministry in Indonesia, he would have protected us from this disaster. This must mean he is not pleased. Does Jesus even accept me as his disciple?* However, before that last thought was finished, I knew I was heading in the wrong direction. As confirmation of that, I heard the words spoken emphatically in my mind, *It is* because *I accept you as my disciple, Bonnie, that I have allowed this child to come to you the way she is. There are many things you don't understand about my kingdom. Learn from her!*

And in this way, the Lord broke through to my understanding. The Lord was not pulling us off the field by giving us a child with special needs, as I had assumed. Rather, the Lord was deepening our call. Obviously, there were things I didn't understand about God's kingdom that the Lord wanted to teach me, but I could only learn as I embraced this special child he was sending us as from him. What was 'sinking my ship' was an unbiblical worldview; I didn't understand how suffering and weakness fit into God's strategy for drawing people to himself. Like the apostle Paul, I was going to learn what God meant when he said, 'My grace is sufficient for you, for my power is made perfect in weakness' (2 Corinthians 12:9).

Another word for 'weakness' could be 'brokenness,' and in his book *Brokenness: How God Redeems Pain and Suffering*, Lon Solomon says, 'Brokenness is not an optional experience for the person who desires God to use them in a mighty way. . . . [It] has been a critical part of the spiritual preparation process for every man and woman whose life God has ever used.'[1] My first steps in this direction required that God expose and dismantle the radical internal commitment to self-sufficiency and pride that lay beneath the surface of my theological training. Four years in seminary had done nothing to dismantle this. It would take a special child to do that. The second step was that I embrace this new and somewhat uncomfortable position of complete dependence on God for everything: future provision, plans, guidance, grace. God had given me a special child and set the direction. What remained was for me to step out in faith.

## Appointed to Bear Fruit

In those months of reflection and waiting, a new understanding began to dawn. I realized, and was coming to accept, that in God's economy, suffering and weakness are often the means God uses to break through to people. Indeed, in his hands, they can serve to break believers in order that they may bring forth greater kingdom fruit in their lives and ministries.

> I believe that there is a high and exalted purpose that explains why God allows heartaches, failures, troubles, and afflictions to enter the lives of godly men and women. This purpose has nothing to do with consequences for negative behaviour or discipline for sin. This exalted purpose involves God's deliberate strategy for producing brokenness in the lives of Christ-followers.[2]

Without a level of brokenness that adequately dismantles the self-life of a believer, Lon Solomon asserts, the believer will never know 'the supernatural power of God' flowing unhindered through their lives.[3]

During this time, Jesus' words spoke emphatically to me, 'You did not choose me, but I chose you and appointed you so that you might go and bear fruit—fruit that will last' (John 15:16). Hebrews 12:7,11 further explained to me: 'Endure hardship as discipline; God is treating you as his children. . . . No discipline seems pleasant at the time, but painful. Later on, however, it produces a harvest of righteousness and peace for those who have been trained by it.' God is about his people producing kingdom fruit, and as I embraced the thought of nurturing and serving a child who would be considered least in this world, people would see something of that fruit. The effort, I was promised, would not be without reward. A harvest of righteousness and peace would be mine if I held fast to the Lord's call. This, indeed, was a special call, but it would require a dependence on the Lord that I did not yet know.

Once I understood what God was doing, the searching questions coming from a place of grief stopped. The tears stopped. I embraced this new direction into brokenness and surrender. It took two months on bed-rest to process the blockages in my understanding caused by having internalized worldly values related to performance and success. What I didn't understand at the time was that the Lord was planting a seed. It was most definitely a mustard seed, the least and smallest of all seeds, yet held potential for kingdom impact (Matthew 13:31–32). And like any planting initiated by God, the Lord would do whatever was needed in order to prepare the soil for maximum fruitfulness. That 'soil' was the soil of my heart, which had become hardened by unspiritual attitudes that lay beneath the surface of my Christian worldview. So, in those two months before Anna's birth, the Lord led me to address heart issues related to pride and prejudice, shame and fear, being judgmental, spiritual brokenness, surrender and trust. In speaking to those issues, the Lord made ready my heart to receive not just the gift of a precious daughter, but also a future ministry.

On December 10, 1999, our daughter, Anna Joy, was born. She was a four-pound, one-month premature baby girl with Down syndrome. She had a heart murmur and a total block between her stomach and intestines (duodenal atresia) that had to be surgically corrected on the third day after she was born. She was in the Neonatal Intensive Care Unit for three weeks, and then she was released to us to bring 'home' to the house rented by the church. We were now a family of four, with our future still in limbo. But there was much to learn in those first two months after Anna's birth. For instance, nursing didn't come easily to Anna Joy or myself, and required a specialist to help me learn creative nursing techniques. Social workers came regularly to the home to train us in simple therapies that we could do with Anna to increase her muscle strength and her cognitive development. 'Stimulate! Stimulate! Stimulate!' the therapists urged us. So, that's what Brent and I did. Our life became one of routines and therapies, and that, in itself, provided stability as we continued to wait on the Lord for the next step. It turned out we didn't have long to wait.

## *The Burning Question*

Within two months of Anna's birth, we felt the first ripple of a breeze blowing in. We received word from our teammates that a new family had arrived on the field who had a seven-year-old daughter with Down syndrome and who was enrolled in the kindergarten class at the Christian international school in our city. Wow! A missionary family had the courage to take a child with a cognitive disability to a developing country! What's more, this child was enrolled in a regular school! New possibilities began forming: If they could do it, why couldn't we? Then our mission pastor's wife further challenged our assumptions: 'If Anna is healthy with no medical conditions that couldn't be handled in Indonesia, why not go back?' Wow, again! But it was true. Anna was healthy in every way. The heart murmur had healed up on its own, and there were no residual effects of the duodenal atresia that had been corrected surgically. Medically, Anna could tolerate a return to Indonesia. Hope began to glimmer.

As Brent and I began to discuss the possibility of a return to Indonesia, however, a question rose up in my heart, a burning question that held growing hope in check until it could be answered. Would it be responsible for us as parents to take a cognitively disabled child away from all the resources available in the United States (therapies, special education, etc.) and bring her to a developing country where there was no guarantee that any resources would be available? Would taking her away from expertise needed for her development be a responsible thing to do? I had to be convinced in my heart that taking Anna away from the experts was the right thing to do for her, and until this question was satisfactorily answered, I put all thoughts of returning to Indonesia on hold.

Within the week, the call came: 'Hello, you don't know me, but I read your letter in our church bulletin announcing the birth of your daughter, Anna Joy. My name is Barbara, and I'm a social worker, and for the last twenty years I have worked as a parent educator for the Montgomery County Social Services Department. I have worked with many children like Anna and their parents, and have seen how, with early intervention, we are able to help move these children further along in their development than if there were no intervention. But, after twenty years serving as a parent educator, I have come to the conclusion that the bottom line for the success of these children in life is good parenting skills.' My heart skipped a beat. To make sure that I had understood correctly, I repeated back to Barbara, word for word, everything that she had just said, turning her last statement into a question, 'And the bottom line for the success of these children in life is good parenting skills?' The voice on the phone said simply, 'Yes, that's right—good parenting skills.' And that was the end of the conversation. To this day, though I have tried to find her, I do not know who this lady was. She was from a supporting church and felt moved to call us to give her expert advice as a social worker. Her input spoke directly to my burning question: her call was the voice of the Lord to me.

## *Green Light! Wait?*

I knew immediately in my spirit that this was the last 'green light' from the Lord that we had been waiting for. If good parenting skills and not necessarily the training and resources of experts were mostly what was needed for Anna's success in life, then we could do that in Indonesia just as well as in America. Rejoicing welled up in my heart. My husband recognized immediately, as well, that the Lord was sending us back to Indonesia. And because the Lord was sending us back, we could have full confidence that he would provide whatever we needed for the job (John 14:13–14). Our plans to return were no longer on hold. Word went out quickly that by the end of the month, the Armistead family would return to their life and ministry in Indonesia.

I would love to say that that's exactly what happened: that we were on the next plane out. But the Lord wasn't finished equipping the vessel that would bear primary responsibility for nurturing and developing this special child on his behalf, namely me. I was still not at the place of spiritual brokenness where Lon Solomon says, 'God crushes all our self-dependence and, in its place, substitutes an utter dependence on God and God alone.'[4] If brokenness is truly God's process to bring every believer to dependence on him, then I was not there yet. It would take a breakdown for me to get to *that* place, and that's exactly what came next.

> God's plan of brokenness . . . is an experience that brings us to the utter end of ourselves. It is an experience where God shatters our self-reliance and self-sufficiency and self-resourcefulness. . . . Through such an experience God forever alters our view of self, God, life, and ministry. In this experience, God delivers the one crushing blow needed to split open a person's hard outer shell like Jesus talks about in John 12. It is after this has been done—and only after this has been done—that God can put in motion the more gentle, gradual, and lifelong part of the process [of brokenness].[5]

This description is the only one I have found that comes anywhere near to explaining what came next for me. My breakdown in the fourth month after Anna's birth was diagnosed as post-partum depression, and 2 percent of women who have postpartum depression have a brief psychotic episode. This is what slammed into me. Suffice to say, I didn't realize how fragile I was, spiritually, emotionally and physically. So when we heard of conflict from the field relating to our unexpected and quick return, I was not able to process it. I stopped sleeping, and by the end of the week, my thinking went from increasingly delusional to psychotic. I should have been hospitalized, but a godly couple who had founded a healing ministry took me into their home until I could stabilize with the help of medication. By the end of the week, I was able to return home, shaky and in pain, but with my mind somewhat restored.

It took about two years before I could say that I was fully recovered from that breakdown, but Brent and I weren't willing to wait for maximum recovery—that could be achieved in Indonesia. We wanted to know what the minimum level of recovery was before we could get on the plane. So, we called the missions pastor at our main sending church and asked him. He admitted that he didn't know much about the subject, but said he thought that one month off of medication with no relapse into psychosis sounded reasonable. It sounded good to us, too, so we got out the calendar, counted out how many days one month on medication and one month off would be, and then bought our return tickets. It was a bold move, but we knew that the Lord was sending us back to Indonesia. One month to the day of being off medication, we were on an airplane headed back to Indonesia. Anna Joy was six months old, and our older daughter, Bethany, had just turned four.

## Evidence of God's Grace in Weakness

At last, we were 'home.' And though I was fragile, I perceived something new pushing up through the broken pieces of my life, and it had to do with the way I related with Indonesians. The invisible barrier of being a wealthy, white Westerner that plagued every relationship I had with my poorer Indonesian neighbours suddenly felt reduced. Of course, in my neighbours' eyes, I was still wealthy, white and foreign, but on the inside, I was changed. Suffering seemed to have dismantled the false self-confidence underlying my high status, and Indonesians now perceived me as being more approachable.

I first noticed this in a friendship I had with a neighbour, Ibu Euyun. Her seventeen-year-old daughter had died unexpectedly from a heart condition, and in her grief, my neighbour experienced a breakdown right about the same time that I experienced mine, though I was in America. As we were talking one day, she acknowledged to me that she still struggled with her thoughts; that they sometimes pulled her down to a place where she was unable to function. I very gently was able to say to her that I knew what that was like. But she responded, 'How can you know what it is like? You're rich. You're American. You come from the richest country in the world. You don't know what it means to suffer.' But, I very gently countered that wealth was in no way a blanket guarantee for a trouble-free life. Something in the way I answered convinced her that what I said was true, and she responded,

'Yes, I suppose you're right. Suffering is part of being human.' Ibu Euyun was Muslim.

This newly gained inner poverty connected me to Indonesians in a deeper, more meaningful way. Shared weakness was like a bridge that connected my heart to theirs, irrespective of race or religion. My own personal experience with suffering had seemingly levelled the playing field, and in another seven years I would also begin to see how Anna's gift of poverty would have an impact on Indonesians.

In the meantime, we discovered an Indonesian therapy centre where Anna was able to receive quality physical therapy. Through our weekly visits to the therapy centre, I began to meet other Indonesian parents who had children with disabilities. Hearing their stories saddened me. One woman shared with me that the reason her baby had Down syndrome was because she had fallen during her pregnancy. Also, she had eaten something that made her very sick, and her pastor informed her that these two things were responsible for her baby having Down syndrome. Needless to say, I took the time to educate her about the facts behind Down syndrome. But I left the centre that day feeling troubled by the ignorance of this Christian pastor's words. His counsel had burdened this young mom with guilt, made all the more heavy because Down syndrome carries profound stigma in Indonesian culture. I sensed the potential for a future ministry of working with parents of children who had disabilities.

## *The Education Venture*

Fast forwarding two years, Anna was accepted into the preschool program of the missionary-affiliated international Christian school in our city. One teacher at the school said to me, 'Anna belongs here. We will do whatever we can to see that she has a good education.' My heart overflowed with gratefulness to God for his provision! Anna was received as a regular student, and the school even provided her with a full-time Indonesian aide. By receiving Anna as a regular student, this Christian school gave our family an invaluable gift and laid a solid academic and social foundation that we have been able to build on over the years. Anna's acceptance enabled her to learn the basic skills necessary to function in mainstream society, and in the time she was there, I learned the vital role that Christian community plays in raising a child with special needs on the mission field. I don't know that Anna would have developed to her fullest potential without the community that the school provided.

However, by the end of first grade, the school informed us that they did not have the expertise or resources to continue to teach Anna in higher grades. The school administrators suggested that 'If you, Bonnie, want to teach Anna yourself and be her aide, we can provide a desk for you in the back of the classroom. In any non-academic activities (calendar time, prayer time, story time, etc.), Anna would be part of the class. But, when the class transitions to core subjects (maths, language arts, science, etc.), she would go back with you to her desk.' Though I couldn't appreciate it at the time, in essence, the school was offering an innovative partnership: a parent-defined and parent-led mixed model of inclusion/homeschooling, in which Anna participated in the non-academic life of the class, but I, as the parent, was responsible for Anna's academic education.

Needless to say, I didn't make it to the end of that meeting before I broke down and cried. What did I know about teaching, let alone from the angle of special ed? I had a BA in political science and an MDiv, but that did not a teacher make! My grief very quickly turned into grumbling. *This is not what I came here to do. I'm a missionary. I didn't come here to homeschool!* Increasingly, I felt hurt that the Lord seemed to be redirecting me 'out' of cross-cultural missions. However, it soon became clear that our options were limited. Either I stepped into this role and became Anna's teacher, or we returned to the States and Anna could be educated through the public school system. There really was no choice at all. The conviction that we had been called to serve in Indonesia was too strong. So, after wrestling for a time with the Lord, I put my sense of entitlement to do 'meaningful work' outside the home on the shelf and added 'Special Ed Teacher' to the list of jobs missionary wives do. It was a case of doing what needed to be done to stay on the field, since that's where God has placed us. As it turns out, we've used this adapted model of inclusion for thirteen years in three different Christian schools. We now hire and train Indonesian university students to be part-time aides for Anna. Not only has this significantly lightened my load, but we have been a Special Ed training ground for Indonesians, and brought additional loving friends into Anna's world.

## *A Kingdom Catalyst*

What I didn't realize at the time was that my training to become a Special Ed teacher-mom had begun. Training was on-the-job, starting with my own child. From second grade, I was in the classroom every day with Anna, facilitating her every endeavour to grow socially and academically. Wonder of wonders, not only did I find I loved this job and that I was good at it, but I also began to see how interacting with Anna pulled good things out of her classmates. These children were learning how to extend grace in the moment to someone who was different from them and who sometimes did things they didn't understand. Here are three vignettes:

> 1. One day in second grade, Anna refused to play dodgeball during P.E. Kirsti, a classmate from Taiwan, marched over to me and demanded, 'Why isn't Anna playing the game?' I explained to Kirsti, 'Anna's favourite colour is red, and only one of the five balls out there is red. Anna would like to throw the red ball, but she can't get it because the game is moving too fast.' Kirsti, who typically showed very little facial expression, thought about that for a moment, and then I saw a twinkle appear in her eyes as understanding dawned. Without another word, Kirsti dashed away and made a beeline for the red ball. She captured it and went straight over to Anna, who threw it. This pattern of Kirsti getting the red ball for Anna continued for the duration of the game. My heart soared to see this breakthrough in relationship—a Taiwanese second-grader stepping into acceptance and serving so that the disadvantaged might be included.
>
> 2. At recess in fourth grade, I saw three fourth-grade boys, two Americans and a Korean, invite Anna to play a game of tag. I immediately suspected the worst, that these boys were looking for a laugh at Anna's expense, but I waited to see what they were up to before I intervened. The game was nothing like what I feared! These boys slowed the game down and found their fun in allowing Anna to catch them whenever she was 'it.' The kindness and gentleness these boys displayed towards one weaker than themselves brought joy to my heart.
>
> 3. Another time, one of the most competitive boys in sixth grade stopped the annual sixth graders versus teachers kickball game because Anna had been skipped in the line-up. He made sure she had a chance to kick the ball.

Of course, all these grace-filled interactions could not have happened without proactively educating Anna's classmates. That job fell to me as Anna's teacher and advocate. Every school year starting in kindergarten, I taught Anna's class a devotion using Aesop's fable, 'The Tortoise and the Hare.' After presenting the fable, I introduced the concept from Genesis that it pleased God to create creatures both fast and slow. From the animal kingdom, I moved on to the human family and made the same point—some people are fast and some are slow by God's design. God is equally pleased with both. This devotion helped to validate students' perceptions that, yes, Anna sometimes did things that didn't make sense to them. But it was okay, because she was slow—God made her that way, and he was not disappointed.

It didn't take long for me to see that Anna's impact was not just limited to her classmates on the playground. Others at the school were also moved. In sixth grade, Anna found the courage to audition for a solo in the elementary Christmas concert. She was nervous the night of the concert and almost backed out. As the time for her solo drew near, the music director, still directing the other students, went to Anna, took her by the hand and led her from the bleachers to the microphone. Anna stood in front of the mic, staring it down, waiting nervously. But she came in exactly on cue, with perfect pitch, and sang her part flawlessly. When Anna finished, an elementary student took her by the hand and led her back to her place in the bleachers. The moment radiated gentleness and kindness. A friend told me later that the young man sitting next to her in the audience, a high school student, broke down crying as soon as Anna started to sing—'blubbering uncontrollably' were her exact words. What was it this young man saw that so touched his heart—something of the beauty of God's kingdom, perhaps?

In the years I've worked on different campuses with Anna as her teacher, I've thought long and hard about Anna's mission: What is it that people see in Anna that acts as a catalyst for goodness to come forth from them as they interact with her? If it's there, something good is released from within people as they engage with Anna. I regularly saw love, joy, patience, kindness, goodness, gentleness and other fruit attributed to the Holy Spirit springing up from within people. What could explain this phenomenon that I was seeing? The answer, I've concluded, is that in Anna's simplicity and innocence, people see something of the beauty of God's kingdom. Furthermore, Jesus said, 'The kingdom of heaven is like yeast that a woman took and . . . worked all through the dough' (Matthew 13:33). In the same way yeast acts as a leavening agent causing dough to rise, so Anna, when integrated into the community, causes people to rise. This is Anna's mission. Anna is a kingdom leavening agent!

*Anna had the same impact on people as yeast has with dough: when integrated into community, she became a catalyst for good. (Used with permission of Bonnie Baker Armistead.)*

It wasn't just in the expat community that Anna had impact. Indonesians were moved as well. Anna was not able to continue at the international school beyond age eight because I didn't have a curriculum that could flex with the teaching style in higher grades. It wasn't working for us to be in the classroom anymore. So, we moved over to an Indonesian school that was started by a Chinese-Indonesian and used a Montessori-type teaching method, which fit Anna's learning style. The founder, Ms Vivi, also wanted to pioneer a Special Ed track as part of her school, and so she personally invited Anna to join. When I attended my first parent-teacher conference, Ms Vivi sat in while Anna's teacher went through her portfolio of achievements. But Ms Vivi wasn't able to stay quiet for long. I could tell she had something important to say because I saw she had tears in her eyes as she waited to speak with me. 'Mrs Bonnie,' she finally broke in, 'we *need* Anna at our school. Indonesian parents have no hope for their children with disabilities, but when they see Anna, that she can read and write, that she loves God and interacts well socially, then for the first time they have a picture of what might be possible for their own child.'

Ms Vivi's words had a profound impact on me that day, not just because here was someone who was thrilled to have my intellectually disabled daughter at their school, but because, in Ms Vivi's words, I discerned Anna's calling. Dr Rick Langer explains that 'Callings are not chosen. Callings are imposed on people . . . [they] are not sought, or found or discovered; they are answered.'[6] God is always the originator of the call. In Anna's case, she did not ask to be born with Down syndrome; she was called to it by her Creator. God had a greater purpose in Anna's special design, a sovereign purpose in line with Jesus' response to his disciples when they asked him in John 9:2, 'Who sinned, this man or his parents, that he was born blind?' Jesus answered, 'Neither . . . but *this happened so that the works of God might be displayed in him*' (v. 3; italics added). Somehow, something of the work of God was going to go on display in Anna's life that would bless Indonesian families, and it had something to do with hope.

*Indonesian parents have no hope for their children with disabilities. Shared weakness gives me an open door to their hearts and facilitates sharing truth about how God perceives their child. (Used with permission of Bonnie Baker Armistead.)*

In a shame-based, status-conscious country like Indonesia, families touched by disability face attitudes in society that project shame and disgrace onto them; that their child is the result of a curse, generational sin or divine judgement. In essence, disability dehumanizes the individual in our context. Ms Vivi named a silent reality for Indonesian parents raising a disabled child—they have no hope. But when they looked at Anna, they were inspired to believe that their child could be more than what was being projected onto them. In Anna, they saw someone who was overcoming her limitations with dignity and grace, and the humanity contained beneath Anna's Down syndrome broke through to them. They could see her humanness, and in so seeing, they could impute that same quality of being human to their own children. They saw no shame in our family, shame that leads many Indonesian families to hide their children away in darkened rooms. That day, I realized that Anna, indeed, had a high calling on her life, a call to carry Down syndrome with dignity and grace. All Anna had to do in order to fulfil her calling was to be herself and to develop to her fullest potential physically, intellectually and spiritually, and in this way she was bringing glory to God. In this way, as well, God was using Anna to draw Indonesians to consider the source of all hope; namely, the truths contained in Scripture about God's love and provision for them, and for their children with disabilities.

*In Anna, Indonesians see someone who is overcoming her limitations with dignity and grace. Anna's academic abilities inspire Indonesians and help them see her humanity through the Down syndrome. (Used with permission of Bonnie Baker Armistead.)*

## An Opportunity of a Lifetime

It is wonderful to know that Anna has this most amazing call on her life, given her by none other than the Creator of the universe. It is also true, however, that in order to fulfil her calling, Anna Joy has needed, and may always need, a person to come alongside her, not only to facilitate her developing to her fullest potential, but also to harvest the fruit that the Lord wants to bring forth in Indonesian hearts as a result of her ministry. For now, that person is me, her mother, chosen and apprenticed to love and to serve one considered least in this world, that God's message of love and salvation might reach those in Indonesia oppressed by the stigma associated with disability.

Along the way we have learned life-transforming lessons that might impact a missionary's longevity on the field in the face of disability. These can be summarised under three areas:

1. *Worldview*. The greatest pain in a parent's life as it relates to their child with special needs often has its source in how they perceive their child in terms of worldly expectations and measures. We can have hidden expectations and aspirations for our children that have been shaped by the world's measures of success and the ability to compete, leaving no room for what God values when it comes to 'success.' Also, if more value is placed on mission work done outside the home, there will be disappointment when the work needed involves homeschooling and extra nurturing *inside* the home.

2. *Calling*. Disability and mission are not incompatible. Indeed, having a disability may actually be an inseparable part of one's call. When you know you're called to do something, then you can have confidence to step out in faith and believe for the impossible. Jesus says, 'You may ask me for anything in my name, and I will do it' (John 14:14). Do we believe that?

3. *God's Sovereign Purposes in Special Needs*. Like the disciples in John 9, we tend to assume the worst about disability. But there is something about the nature of disability that puts us in a position to experience a move of God in our lives. We should all ask: What might the Lord want to do in our life and in the lives of our family through disability that might display his work and kingdom values?

Our journey to fully embracing this call has been long and arduous, fraught with questions as I've learned to follow and trust 'him who is invisible' (Hebrews 11:27). Make no mistake: raising a child with disabilities on the field may be one of the hardest and most time-consuming investments you will ever make in your life, but it holds great potential for kingdom impact on the people around you, and it brings glory and pleasure to God as you place yourself in a position to experience his provision and grace. Disability and weakness are, indeed, a high calling. But my experience shows that in God's hands they are an invitation to participate with God in doing ministry his way—by faith through weakness and a willingness to be led by him into the unknown. What a life! What an adventure! What a gracious God we serve!

CHAPTER 4

# Unformed yet Ordained

J M Paul
United States

'Your eyes saw my unformed body; all the days ordained for me were written in your book before one of them came to be.'

(Psalm 139:16)

Motherhood and the world of disability found me when I least expected it. My story begins six months into marriage. My husband, John, and I had met on the mission field, and soon after our marriage we made our first home in a bungalow atop tea plantations in rural Northeast India. We had hearts aware of our great God, who moved heaven and earth to rescue his people, and we were passionate about spreading that truth to this little corner of the world. We imagined ourselves doing that through providing education and healthcare. I had trained as a nurse, worked in obstetrics nursing, and studied tropical nursing at the London School of Tropical Medicine. I was fervent to see women freed from the bondage of slavery to sin as well as the bondage of oppression that poor health care and societal injustices had burdened them with. My husband was a well-trained and passionate psychiatrist with a vision of revolutionizing mental healthcare in rural North India. Both passions and skill sets were good, and God-authored I believe; however, often our plans became delusions of grandeur, and we had no plan of being distracted from our goals.

I had been in India about three years at this point, and was aware of the vast population affected by disability. I had seen leprosy, the effects of polio, and disabilities that left many stigmatized and homeless. I was aware of the huge array of other conditions that surrounded me on the overcrowded streets and heaving slums. However, I kept those affected by disability at a distance emotionally. Sure, I would sit with the family affected by leprosy. To see an aged woman affected by leprosy, rolling out chipati with misshapen hands, pained me. But I did not think I had any role in caring for her beyond visits and prayers. I would hold her hands and play with her children. I volunteered in hospitals and cared for the sick. Seeing a boy whose gait was broken by polio, who was unable to walk due to the deformities in his legs, ached my heart and made me cry out to God, 'Why?' But it did not beckon me forward to engage with him. I kept a certain distance.

So to imagine myself inviting a child with a disability into my family was far from possible. I would go to sleep at night afraid of ever having a child born with a diagnosis or medical needs. I found myself afraid of how that would change my life and, dare I say, 'mess up' my life. Little did I know how wrong I was. For I was about to be grafted into this community of people, and I would soon see that they dwelt on holy ground. This community would draw me nearer to God and his kingdom than I knew was possible.

On 18 September my first son was born. It was the day before my six-month wedding anniversary. He was born to a local tribal woman, alone, in our little mission hospital. He had a genetic condition that left him with significant physical deformities. He had no eyelids, no fingers, severely webbed legs, a cleft palate and lip, as well as an absent nose. His appearance left everyone in the delivery room—medical staff and birth mother—shocked and in disbelief. His mother had received no prenatal care and simply came to the hospital for delivery. He was abandoned at the hospital by his birth family, who were too saddened and overwhelmed by his condition, and who saw him as a spiritual curse. When I first met him, he was lying alone in an infant warmer bed at the hospital. His eyes were perpetually open because he had no eyelids to close them. Due to the webbing of his legs, he could not uncoil his body into a comfortable position. He lay in the bed, curled up, with his eyes searching the room constantly.

My husband and I prayed for this little one. We invited others to pray. We sent his picture and the bit of his story we knew to loved ones around the world. The hospital staff prayed, and hundreds around the world joined in, emailing prayer notes and letters to this precious baby boy. We prayed for an idea of how to care for him. I searched Scripture for guidance, longing for an answer. I came to India prepared for a lot of things, but a baby this disfigured and abandoned in a hospital, and all the resulting ethical implications, were not on my radar. We sought medical advice and we continued to pray. Meanwhile, this little baby had sadly become a sort of entertainment to the local villagers. People would come by asking to see 'that baby' or questioning if 'it' still was alive. They wanted pictures and they wanted updates, but no one wanted to hold him. There was no respect for the babe and no concern for his life. He was different, and that meant that everyone felt they had a right to see him, yet his personal rights were never considered.

I read and reread David's words in Psalm 139 where he writes, 'your eyes saw my unformed body.' I had read this passage so many times, yet never had I paid attention to that verse. This time, it pierced my heart. God's word is alive and active and it pierces bone and marrow as it penetrates these feeble hearts of ours. When I questioned this boy's condition, God's word answered with, 'your eyes saw my unformed body.' This baby was unformed from head to toe. But God saw him. God formed him. God wove his existence into being, unformed as it was. And that Abba God saw fit to breathe life into this little one's lungs. This was a life, and it was good.

We named him Adam so that he would not be known as 'that baby,' or worse, 'that thing' any more. God made that first man, Adam, in his image and saw that it was good. Adam was a respected and known name across all major religions of that area, and it spoke strength and dignity and truth.

We wrestled over the implications of an abandoned baby in rural India. We questioned what the best response was to his life. Would he live long? What sort of medical care did he need? Did it even make sense to repair such a broken body? Would he go blind without eyelids? Most likely, he would.

The questions were overwhelming. Then we imagined his existence in the confines of a rural mission hospital. Staff would come and go and so would his care. He would be moved from empty patient bed to empty patient bed without any semblance of normality, and far from any notion of family. Is such a life even worthwhile? We had no idea we were to be a critical part of Adam's rescue by our Abba God.

Meanwhile, my husband and I had been doing a Tim Keller study on the book of Romans. We had crossed Romans 8:15, which says, 'you have received the Spirit of adoption as sons, by whom we cry, "Abba! Father!"' (ESV). When Adam was a couple of days old, my husband came home from work and exclaimed: 'We were Adam.'

I responded, 'And that means . . . ?'

'We were Adam, spiritually, before Christ. We were disfigured by our sin, we were orphans (John 14:18), and we were destined for death (Romans 3:23). But God, in his great love, adopted us. He rescued us and made us his sons and daughters. It was not easy. It cost him everything, but he did it.'

So, if we believed God is who he says he is, and if he, our God, gave this radical display of love and redemption for us, and if he calls us to be imitators of himself (Ephesians 5:1), then what response did we have except to adopt this little one into our family? How could we say that we came to tell people about a God of love and yet respond in the same way as those who do not know God by rejecting this little life?

We decided that day: we would pursue Adam's adoption. We became his foster parents and started the difficult medical journey that lasted for nearly five years. We learned his diagnosis, and we swallowed back tears. He had an extremely rare condition called Bartsocas-Papas Popliteal Pterygium Syndrome. We heard the prognosis: he would not live two months. The geneticists who diagnosed him encouraged us to slowly reduce feeding Adam and provide palliative care. This advice came on the same day that all of his scans came back and revealed a normal brain, heart, liver, kidneys and lungs. When we asked how he would die and why we should reduce feedings we were simply told 'we do not know enough about this condition, but we do know that they do not live long.' We decided we would continue to feed him and love him and let our God, the Author of life, decide how long his life should be.

It was demanding. My work as a nurse stopped completely and my husband had to lower his expectations for work goals. We heard from a major medical hospital in the US that they had a team of doctors who could provide the care needed for Adam's reconstructive surgeries and that he should have a 'normal' life if he could get through these surgeries. So we traveled to the US, and Adam made it through days of medical investigations. All the specialists saw him and gave their predictions and what they thought would be best for Adam. Meanwhile, Adam's personality started to blossom and people commented especially on how his eyes were talking constantly.

We watched fourteen surgeries come and go. We watched as Adam learned how to sit up, and we heard, with the accompaniment of angels, when Adam laughed his first laugh. We laughed when we learned his cleft lip would be repaired on Valentine's Day (because doesn't God love us so tenderly, and doesn't he coordinate lips to be fixed on that day we all love to kiss those near us?). We welcomed little brothers into Adam's family and saw him learn how to love them. We watched Adam surpass all expectations and leave us in this constant state of awe.

There were tough nights and angry nights. There were nights when we questioned if it is all worth it. Those were nights when he fought sickness and we fought for sanity. It was hard, and we wrestled. But our God picked us up again and again. He filled us with himself, and he taught us to love. He has been an ever-present help in times of trouble. He never leaves nor forsakes. He knows how to take 'foolish' and seemingly impossible things, like a baby given two months to live, and shame the wisdom of this world and this mama.

After I had become his foster mom, and was days away from being his adoptive mom, I remember lying in bed and trusting God with this question: *Can I raise a dying child?*

His still small voice replied, *You, too, are dying.*

Yes, our spirits will live, but this body, it is fading. 'Though outwardly we are wasting away, yet inwardly we are being renewed day by day' (2 Corinthians 4:16). After all, didn't Solomon tell us, 'There is a time for everything, and a season for every activity under the heavens: a time to be born and a time to die' (Ecclesiastes 3:1–2)? And we are told that 'All people are like grass, and all their faithfulness is like the flowers of the field. . . . The grass withers and the flowers fall, but the word of our God endures forever' (Isaiah 40:6,8).

We are eternal beings. We will one day see all things made new! The notion that we are all dying is not fatalistic. Each year that passes I see changes in my own body. We all age and no one knows if she is guaranteed tomorrow.

Do I love Adam or any of my family and friends less because of unavoidable death?

No. I love them deeply in this moment.

Then why should I question loving, adopting and caring for this precious boy, because the medical advice was to let him die?

We do not know what tomorrow holds. But I know who holds it, and I know this moment. I know Jesus. I know what love is. I know God's word. And, after all, the word of the Lord endures forever.

Flesh fades like grass, but the word endures.

The word gives me the strength I need to love Adam.

And now I see it. We can abandon delusions of grandeur and submit to this God who turns our notions of good upside down and uses fools to shame the wise. We can trust this God and know that he came and he changed the world through the shame of the cross. He sees our unformed bodies, and yet he loves us. And this same God calls us to be imitators of himself, equipping us with all that we need to carry out his work of redemption in this broken world. And this God can use little babies whom many may see as worthless and weak, and bring his kingdom through them. He takes those with disabilities and shows all of us 'able ones' that we need each other.

Adam helped me learn to see that suffering and inability are often the means by which God breaks through to us, humans who so often rely on comfort and ability. I, most of all, relied on my comfort and ability. I had a one-course track to serving the Lord and sharing his message of hope to the nations. I would have never imagined that becoming a mother and caregiver to a child with significant needs would be one of the main channels through which God would share his light to the world around me. He surprised me with how great an impact he made through Adam. Not only were the lives of those around us in India affected, but we hear stories nearly daily of people around the world who have heard Adam's story and been changed.

*A pit stop on a long drive in north India. Travel with Adam was always more challenging and more beautiful. Adam is pictured with his parents and little brother. (Used with permission of J M Paul.)*

Overwhelming love and support poured in with our decision to adopt Adam. However, there were a few loud, strong voices that discouraged us, and their voices lingered for many years. A well-known missionary physician told us Adam would take us away from the mission field. Another missionary physician, who had a child with a disability, told us that he would never choose that life again for himself and that we were making a ridiculous decision. Another advised us to find an orphanage and leave Adam there, as his presence in our family would strain our marriage and distract us from our ministry. I love each of those individuals dearly; however, their words brought doubt and anxiety. Thankfully, the voice of the Lord overpowered all of them in my mind. He spoke still and small, reminding me, 'I use the foolish things of the world to shame the wise.' God would turn that acclaimed wisdom inside out and show us the paradoxes of his kingdom.

Because the reality is that our marriage was strengthened through Adam's adoption. When you lose your life you find it, and we found our life in losing careers and dreams, and choosing to love and advocate for Adam.

Although the Lord's voice remained strong, other people's opinions affected us in some ways. We had moments of anxiety when their words would come back to our minds and we would think that perhaps this was too difficult for us. We would grow worried about Adam's future and rising financial needs and how to manage life in India with such significant medical needs. But when we fixed our eyes above and we remembered from where our help does come, our gaze steadied and our hearts rested. Our help comes from God above. As Paul wrote in Philippians 1:6, 'He who began a good work in you will carry it on to completion.'

There were also the reactions that we received in public, and they were often the hardest. In India, where those who look different are often stigmatized, Adam always drew stares. We heard hurtful comments and we had to block people from taking pictures without asking. There were times when I took on a 'mother bear' mentality and anticipated rude remarks with a bitter heart. My heart grew jaded, and instead of looking expectantly on a chance to love others and share Adam's story with hope and joy, I grew easily irritated as I blocked his face from onlookers.

When people's opinions and words influenced me more than God's words towards Adam, my heart was hard and skeptical. However, when I renewed my heart and mind and set my mind on things above, I was given eyes that looked at Adam and saw beauty, purpose and value. Once I got to that place, it changed everything. For when we set our eyes on things above, we gain a perspective from above. And a perspective from above sees beauty in ashes. A perspective from above shames wise men with foolish things. A perspective from above sees an unformed baby abandoned in a rural village in India as a life with value and purpose. This type of perspective, from above, expects mountains to be moved and God's kingdom to come down, on earth as it is in heaven, when weak people rely on a strong God.

Mountains were moved and his kingdom came down as his will was done in the life of our little Adam. Instead of taking us from the mission field, Adam's life expanded our mission field. We began to see others in new ways. We learned how to relate to people in different ways. Even though Adam never walked, his story has traveled continents and nations. Even though Adam never spoke, his story has echoed from mouths on platforms high and in living rooms and rooftops across the world. Adam did not take our mission; instead, God brought Adam into our life to turn our idea of mission upside down and to take his gospel love to places we would never have gone otherwise.

We have been able to share God's love in hospital waiting rooms across the US and on news channels and radio broadcasts across the world. Adam's story has been splayed across the front pages of newspapers and has been spread virally on all forms of social media. The activist and Star Trek actor George Takei once tweeted 'baby Adam is fortunate' with a link to Adam's story. That is an avenue of impact that we never even dreamed of having. But our God is one of paradoxes who takes foolish things to shame the wise. He takes a life we deem worthless and changes the world and our own hearts.

One of our biggest fears, which was only validated by the words and concerns of many others, was what our life in India would look like now as we had a child with significant medical needs alongside of us. We imagined that it would remove our ability to serve and distract us from 'missions.' We were so terribly wrong. Adam paved a road for us. Adam's life brought connection. Hurting people would see Adam and be comforted. Jaded people would hear Adam's story and their walls would come down. Skeptics would watch Adam and his dad play and laugh together and they would weep. The impact that we had as a couple exponentially grew when we adopted Adam. We saw the name of Jesus go forth in places and in ways we had never seen before. We saw a young woman's faith transformed as we brought Adam into our family. We had been reading through Scripture with her for months before we met Adam. She was reading through John, and she exclaimed, 'When I read this book, it is as though I was blind and now I can see for the first time!' When we called her and told her about Adam, she was anxious to meet him and help care for him. Her heart was softened by seeing the love of God displayed in the adoption of a child who had been seen as a curse. A few months after his adoption, she placed her faith in Jesus. The word of God and the picture of his redemptive love for mankind in the life of Adam made the main impact on her decision, and it was humbling to be a part of that.

Instead of taking us away from the mission field, Adam expanded the mission field around us. Adam's life gave us eyes to see those previously unseen by us. We started to be more aware of needs within the community of those with disabilities around the world. A group of inclusive playgrounds have been built across rural North India in memory of Adam. We also learned to redefine 'missions.' We learned that 'missions' is not defined by life in a remote missions hospital running medical camps and teaching nursing students. Yes, that is one way to serve in mission, but that is not the only way. We had tunnel vision, and the Lord used Adam to expand our vision beyond what we could have asked or imagined. Mission is a life laid down. Whether you are in a place across the world from your home or with those you have known all your life, when you lay your life down you display the love of Christ, and that is mission.

After Adam's first set of surgeries in the US—which included major leg surgery, eyelid reconstruction, cleft lip repair, g-tube placement, ostomy bag placement and tracheostomy placement—we had to return to India as his medical visa gave us only six months in the US. When we returned to India I was six months pregnant with Adam's brother, Elliot. We survived a long summer together, Adam and I. A first-time pregnant mom in the heat of an Indian summer along with a 10-month-old son with multiple medical needs that interfered with his ability to tolerate heat made for quite a sight! Adam and I spent many hours each day in our bathtub with cold water. I grew Elliot and cared for Adam while John made our home ready and grew his psychiatry practice.

A few weeks before Elliot was born, John had a pastor come to his office concerned about a young girl named Hadassah who had recently started coming to his church. She had been sold for labour as a child, married as a young teenager to an older man, and had since battled anger and depression. During one episode of anger she heard voices telling her to end her life. She attempted suicide multiple times in different ways, and the last time was by covering herself in kerosene and lighting herself on fire. Her husband found her burning, put out the fire, and rushed her to the hospital. He then left her at the hospital with some money and never returned. After months of treatment in the hospital with multiple surgeries, grafts and therapies, Hadassah walked out alive with burns on 70 percent of her body. Having survived, she was now alone and without a clue as to how to cope with such physical brokenness. She lived in different shelters for a year until she found a roommate in a village near where we lived.

She started attending a local church and when her pastor heard her history, he wanted to connect her to a counsellor. That is how we first met Hadassah. John saw her that day in the clinic and she then joined us for lunch. I still remember her that first day. She was covered from head to toe in layers of dark cloth in the heat of summer. She was ashamed of her scars and tired of the looks people gave her when walking down the street, so she hid all that she could. John told Hadassah about Adam before she arrived at our home, but upon meeting Adam, she fell apart. She wept, prayed out loud, removed her head covering to expose her scars, and she reached out to pick him up. She held him close, and as he looked at her, there was a moment of shared suffering and understanding unlike anything I have witnessed. Hadassah asked for more of Adam's story that day and wept as she said, 'If God has a purpose for Adam's life even though he was born like this, then he must still have a plan for my life too.' Hadassah started to visit us a couple of times a week and eventually moved in with us. She lived with us for three years and she and Adam had a deep love for one another. After a couple of weeks of spending time with Adam, Hadassah stopped wearing her head coverings and started dressing without worrying about covering up her scars. After a couple of years, we watched Hadassah grow into a confident young woman who was comfortable in her skin and her story. She and Adam had a friendship that ran deep because they both had tasted deep suffering and social rejection.

If it were not for Adam and his story, I wonder if we would have connected with Hadassah at all. Through Adam, the playing field was levelled and we could relate to her in a way that we could not have otherwise. Because of Adam's scars, Hadassah felt safe to show her own scars. Now, five years later, Hadassah is thriving and shares her story with others who have been through hard things. And we see God's word again, living and active, as he comforted us and Adam in our troubles, so that we could comfort Hadassah in hers. As Hadassah receives comfort, she herself finds the freedom and grace to comfort others.

Another glimpse of God's faithfulness in using Adam's brokenness to comfort those around us was when a young man, paralyzed from falling off a ladder, came into our hospital in India. His name was Kumar and he was not quite twenty years old when he fell. He had been battling depression and was lying silently in the patient ward with his parents. He would not speak to any doctors or nurses and was refusing treatment. That evening we took Adam on a walk around the hospital campus and stopped by Kumar's bed in the male ward. His parents were silently squatting eating their dinner. Adam was about two years old at this point and not the most social of souls. He was temperamental and irritable with anyone except those he knew well. In addition to that, it was hot, and Adam's condition prevented him from sweating, so the heat was especially intense for him. Therefore, we were not expecting much of an interaction between Kumar and Adam, but thought we would visit him after work hours to check in on him.

Kumar eyed Adam and invited him to the bed where he was lying. Adam sat right next to Kumar's face and touched him first with his little hand that had no fingers. He felt all around his face and Kumar snuck a smile. Then, much to everyone's surprise, Adam leaned down full on Kumar's face and kissed him with his slobbery, surgically repaired mouth. Kumar, who was unable to move due to his paralysis, simply had to receive the kiss from Adam. He could not object or turn away. When Adam pulled away, Kumar had tears falling down his face and his parents were weeping off to the side as well. I think it was the total brokenness of Adam's two-year-old body that really touched their hearts, and to see his complete vulnerability with their son in his own need left them speechless.

The exchange between these two boys was so sacred. What a kind God we have that he not only walks with us through our suffering, but he becomes the suffering one, so that our pain is not the end of the story. What a gentle God we have that he never leaves us nor forsakes us in our pain, but he is with us always. Not only that, but he chooses to use our pain to comfort others, to bring glory to his name and to make us more like him.

We are now in a new season with our Adam. His beautiful life came to a sudden, to us, end in June 2016. We were temporarily back in the US in order to gain Adam's US citizenship for insurance and medical reasons. He had started school, was walking on prosthetics and was regularly surprising all of us with his strength and skills. He was nearing his fifth birthday and we were often taken aback as we remembered how the Lord had brought us so far with this little one. He had two adoring little brothers who shared a room with him and followed him throughout the house. Adam was playful and thriving when he suddenly became very ill and fought a difficult last week in a paediatric ICU, before passing away one week after his admission. Our family is still recovering in some ways from the loss of Adam. Having him in our home was a taste of heaven on earth every day. It was a daily miracle when a boy who was told he would be blind could see; a boy whose adoptive parents were told to stop feeding him was growing and thriving. He was a daily reminder that God is the author of life and the restorer of broken things.

We are learning now to taste heaven on earth in different ways. We are tasting it in God's presence with our grieving sons. We are tasting it in memories shared by people who loved Adam. Adam is gone, but our Lord continues to work in our home in heavenly ways, and we are thankful. The verse from Psalm 139 that opens with 'your eyes saw my unformed body' has a refrain that I overlooked until well after Adam passed away. David wrote, 'All the days ordained for me were written in your book before one of them came to be,' and that now brings me deep hope. Adam's life and death were

*Christmas Eve 2015. We had no idea it would be our last Christmas with Adam. He always brought extra magic to the Christmas season because of his love for twinkle lights. He is pictured here with his two younger brothers. (Used with permission of J M Paul.)*

authored by the same loving God who embraced suffering so that our suffering would not be in vain. His death was not a surprise to the God who authored its beginning. And though some see his story as over, his legacy and testimony live on, and are a daily reminder to our family that losing your life is finding your life. Adam's dependency on us for physical care is a reminder of our dependency on our Father. And his life of ministry, simply by living in his disability and breathing the air God breathed into his lungs, in the midst of struggle and pain, remind us to walk out the lives God has given us. It is a reminder that instead of cursing the weaknesses that we have, or those with weaknesses around us, we can embrace the weaknesses and see how our good God can use them for his redemptive purposes.

Adam's death was hard for many reasons. One of the most significant reasons was the deep loss of such a tangible miracle in our lives. Adam loved us and gave us so much joy, and his life brought joy and light wherever he went. If I had been able to write Adam's story, I would not have ended it so soon. That is the truth of my heart. It is hard for me to understand why our

Lord would want to end his life when it seemed in many ways to be only beginning. But this verse quiets my restless heart and mind. All of Adam's days were ordained for him before one of them even came to be. They were written in God's story, and his is the story that will last forever and ever. My story and my mind are finite and limited. God's story is infinite and without end.

I trust his story. I trust that what he did with Adam's life on earth was good and powerful and I trust that this is not the end of the story. I saw our Lord work good through the brokenness of Adam's body; therefore I trust that I will see him continue to work good through brokenness in the rest of our journey in missions. Our hearts have certainly changed and our eyes see people differently. We serve with a bend towards the broken as we walked a broken road. We discovered that our Saviour walked it too. As we seek to serve, we keep our eyes fixed above, on where our help comes from.

There is a deep joy and longing ache that comes in sharing the life of our beautiful son Adam and the impact he had for the gospel during his nearly five years on earth. Adam transformed both my husband's and my heart and mission to look away from ourselves and our short-sighted views of changing the world. Adam's life caused us to turn our gaze to the offensive and paradoxical reality of a wooden cross with a perfect, yet broken Saviour King splayed across it. He is a King who gave his perfect self to save a broken world and restore community at its deepest roots. Community change happens when we realize that our neediness makes us all disabled, but that we have a King who is able. He is able to work through broken people to restore broken things. This profound insight through the journey with our precious son has been central to our mission journey thus far. When we return to the mission field, we will go out in mission with our hearts in a different place from when we first went out seven years ago. Adam has taught us about God's mission, and the humble, often broken, role we play in that mission. And in so much that Adam has taught us about ourselves and our mission, Adam's legacy will live on in our mission journey and in the many others whom God challenged and changed through Adam. In the days God ordained, he has worked beyond our imagination in Adam's life and, in painful but beautiful ways, he continues to work through his death. We know that this is not the end of the story.

CHAPTER 5

# Called and Equipped through Paraplegia

Barry Funnell
The Word for the World Bible Translators
United Kingdom

I was in my second year of dental studies in South Africa and life could not have been going better for me. I was on the way to becoming a rich dentist, living in luxury, enjoying overseas holidays, playing golf on Wednesday afternoons and not having a care in the world, so I thought!

A friend of mine invited me to join him in a student prank one night. Our plan was to create a stir at midnight in a gym hall attached to a women's student residence by romping around on all the gymnastic equipment in order to wake up all the girls, and then to get away before we were caught. We climbed onto the roof and I removed a few clips holding down a skylight, but it would not budge. As we turned to leave and look for another way in, I pretended to dummy-kick the skylight cover, but then my foot went through it, my ankle twisted as I tried to pull myself back, and I went plummeting through the skylight, landing with a sickening thud on the solid concrete floor below.

As I lay helplessly on the floor I heard the anguished pleas from my friend beckoning me to get up and get out of there because we were going to get into big trouble. All he heard from the darkness below was, 'My back, my back hurts . . . !' My friend dashed off to get some medical students from his residence to try to help get me stable and out of the gym hall. Fortunately, a decision was soon made to call an ambulance, and the ambulance men climbed in through a window, got me onto a spinal board and passed me out through the window at around 1:00 a.m.

After about two hours I regained consciousness. I had a neck brace on and my back felt very sore. I was told I had broken my back, and was shown an X-ray of the fracture. I reached down under the blanket in the hospital bed to touch my leg and it felt like I was touching a dead leg. I had no feeling in my legs and could not move them at all. I asked the doctor, 'Will I be able to walk again?' He said it was still too early to tell and my fracture did not look too bad. He also said, because I was so muscular (I had been doing training with weights for several years), the vertebrae may have been badly displaced, and damaged the spinal cord, but they had been pulled back into reasonable alignment, so we would have to wait and see.

I tried to process all this information and drifted in and out of consciousness. I clearly remember having a divine encounter with God. He reminded me of a sermon my dad had preached from Luke 12:20. 'But God said to him, "You fool! This very night your life will be demanded from you. Then who will get what you have prepared for yourself?"' It was as if eternity flashed before me. I felt terrified and thought, *Will I stand before God's judgment throne tonight and give an account of my life?* I felt I had nothing to show in terms of spiritual things. I had never witnessed about Christ's love to a single person. I was too cool for that! I knew I was not rich towards God, as it goes on to say in Luke 12:21.

## A Life-Changing Turning Point

I had grown up in a Christian home, with a loving father and mother. I always had enough food, and warm clothes to wear. We went on two annual holidays, usually to a beach resort, and were all in very good health. My brothers and I would play rugby or cricket in our back yard with some friends for hours after school. I was a popular kid in my class, and performed well academically, although I was known by my teachers to be rather mischievous and disruptive. I was baptized by my father at the age of fourteen and enjoyed attending church, youth camps and church family camps.

But at the age of sixteen I had my first serious girlfriend and began to wander away from God. I became very preoccupied with sport, friends, body-building and worldly things, and became more and more self-centred. I also became the clown of the class and enjoyed being the centre of attention in my senior school days. I often made jokes at other people's expense and was very insensitive to others' needs or feelings. When I passed my interview for a place at Witwatersrand University in Johannesburg to study dentistry, and achieved the required grades, pride entered in. Although I attended church, I balked at the idea of giving my all to Jesus. An expression of my dad's that I did not like was: 'If you don't crown Jesus Lord of all, you don't crown him at all!' By the time I reached my second year of dentistry all

I could think of was myself, my pleasures and how I was going to become a very rich man. My girlfriend's father had started building a beautiful townhouse for my girlfriend and me to move into, and he had promised to build a dental practice for me too.

As I pondered all these things that night, lying paralyzed in my hospital bed, I recommitted my life fully to God. I repented of my self-centredness, my wrongdoings, my pride and my running away from God and his plan for my life. I asked God to forgive me and to pick up the broken pieces of my life and use me as he saw fit. I told God that if he would spare my life, I would serve him with all my heart. I felt embarrassed before God that I had so often endangered myself due to seeking an adrenaline rush and wanting to impress others, instead of living my life for him.

No movement or feeling returned to my legs, and due to my spinal cord being completely severed, I lost control of my bladder and bowel. I had to face the prospect of spending the rest of my life in a wheelchair. A major part of my rehabilitation was gaining the ability to empty my bladder via self-catheterization, and also to evacuate my bowel manually. I can say this was, and still is, the most difficult and awkward aspect of paraplegia.

As well as physical and medical aspects, including the searing, ongoing pain caused by a broken back, there were also emotional and psychological effects from the accident, and of facing a future with a major disability. Local pastors came to visit and also to pray for me. Most of them were really sensitive and prayed for physical healing, but also prayed that I would know the love, grace and patience to deal with my current circumstances, which can only come from the Lord.

## Encountering God's Word

The most profound help and encouragement during these early and difficult days of rehabilitation came from my Bible. I would spend hours each day reading chapter after chapter to find comfort and solace. I began to come to know God and his love for me more intimately than ever before. Well-meaning people would come to visit and counsel me, but I can truly testify that their words paled into insignificance in comparison with the power of God's word which began to transform my mind. Romans 8 had the most profound impact on my life and it is still my favourite chapter in the Bible. I experienced God's unconditional love through reading Romans 8:39—'neither height nor depth, nor anything else in all creation, will be able to separate us from the love of God that is in Christ Jesus our Lord.' 'Anything else' included a fall from a height, a wheelchair, a spastic bladder and bowel. I felt God saying to me that he loves me unconditionally. The world dislikes disability because it cannot cope with the inconvenience and 'ugliness' of it, but God looks beyond these. His love is unconditional.

Romans 8:28 says, 'And we know that in all things God works for the good of those who love him, who have been called according to his purpose.' I began to see that God can even use my disability to glorify him, and that he can cause it to work for my good and the good of others. I saw that I could be used by God to encourage those around me who were suffering with disability. The grace of God and his love began to shine out of my life. The hospital staff in the spinal unit began to put the 'difficult' patients next to my bed, so that I could encourage them and help them through their depression or anger. God began to give me a love for people around me, and a desire to tell them of his love.

I was greatly encouraged by Romans 8:37, 'No, in all these things we are more than conquerors through him who loved us,' and Philippians 4:13, 'I can do all this through him who gives me strength.' I read these verses with new meaning. Even in paraplegia, I am more than a conqueror. If there is nothing to overcome or conquer, then how can I be more than a conqueror? I began to rely more and more on his strength to get me through each day. Ironically, Psalm 18:29, 'with my God I can scale a wall,' really encouraged me. It was something I enjoyed in my able-bodied days, scaling a wall higher than my friends could, but now even learning to push up a small step in my wheelchair, or learning to balance so I could go down a step, was a challenge I could do with God. God truly became like a best friend to me, and I enjoyed talking to him throughout the day, and asking him for help even in the small things.

I learned to relate to God as my father, as in Romans 8:15, 'the Spirit you received brought about your adoption to sonship. And by him we cry, "*Abba*, Father."' I felt God's unconditional love as a son of his. He understood my weaknesses and frailties, and knew my real needs. I could rely on him to take care of me whatever the circumstances, as in Romans 8:26, 'In the same way, the Spirit helps us in our weakness. We do not know what we ought to pray for, but the Spirit himself intercedes for us through wordless groans.'

I spent three months being rehabilitated in hospital and then had to face the question of whether I could continue with dentistry. The night after my professor said he doubted I would be able to do so, I lay weeping on my bed in desperation, and cried out to God to speak to me. I asked what job he wanted me to do for the rest of my life. I reached out for my treasured Bible, through which God had spoken to me so intimately for the past three months. I prayed, *Dear God, speak to me, as you did to the boy Samuel. I want to hear your voice and not just turn to a Scripture. Please speak to me.* No audible voice came, but a Scripture reference came as clear as a bell into my mind, 2 Timothy 3:17. My heart began to pound in my chest, and I wondered if this really was God speaking. Slowly I opened my Bible to verse 17: 'so that the servant of God may be thoroughly equipped for every good work.' I knew from that moment, without a doubt, that God wanted me to serve him full-time. God wanted me to be 'a man of God,' while the dental professor was saying I was not good enough to continue my dentistry. I had desperately been trying to be 'a man of the world,' to be accepted and praised by people of the world, but the people of the world were now rejecting me as useless. I found I could no longer enjoy those worldly things I had aspired to. But God was saying to me, *I want you to be a man, my man, a man of God. I want you to be thoroughly equipped for every good work. You are not useless to me. I want you in my service!*

Without hesitation I said yes to God. He had spoken to me through his word. I read 2 Timothy 3:16, which says, 'All Scripture is God-breathed and is useful for teaching, rebuking, correcting and training in righteousness.' I knew that I would need to study God's word more and more to be thoroughly equipped. I read a little further on to 2 Timothy 4:2, which says, 'Preach the word; be prepared in season and out of season.' From then on it didn't matter so much whether I would continue studying dentistry or not. I knew that God had a bigger and more wonderful plan for my life. I knuckled down and studied very hard over my summer holidays, spending many revitalizing hours in prayer and in God's word, which had become like a survival pill for my life. The Bible is truly living and active as it says in Hebrews 4:12.

God opened the doors for me to continue studying dentistry and I received much help and encouragement from my parents. But now, through my experience of disability, Jesus had become everything in my life. I took 2 Timothy 4:2, 'Preach the word,' which can also be translated as 'Do the work of an evangelist,' very seriously. I witnessed to students on campus during lunch breaks and led many to the Lord. I found people very willing to talk to me about matters of faith. I believe my wheelchair disarmed them. They would often ask what happened to me and I was able to tell them how my accident drew me to the Lord and how he was sustaining me each day.

Instead of trying to be the clown of the class and draw attention to myself, God began to give me a love for others, and also a strong sense of eternity. A poem by C T Studd motivated me greatly: 'Only one life, 'twill soon be passed, only what's done for Christ will last.'[1] John 9:4 also inspired me: 'As long as it is day, we must do the works of him who sent me. Night is coming, when no one can work.' This really gave me a sense of urgency about my life and use of time. I felt I needed to talk to people about their need for Christ—today, and not tomorrow. I may never see a particular person again, so I had better share my faith in Christ with them now, and not delay. Perhaps if I did not speak to them, they might go to a Christ-less eternity.

My fourth and fifth years as a dental student were spent doing dental work on patients, and this was a wonderful opportunity for me to witness to them. Generally I would briefly explain why I was in a wheelchair, as many people would ask me what happened. This would always lead me to communicate how much God meant to me and how he used the accident in my life to draw me closer to him. Dental patients are 'a captive audience' so to speak! There is even a dentist's psalm: Psalm 81:10, 'Open wide your mouth and I will fill it.' I would share the love of Christ with them, and after finishing my work on their teeth, I would ask them if they wanted to spend more time chatting or if they wanted to pray to receive Christ. Another advantage is that they would come for multiple visits so I could follow up with them on previous conversations. I do believe my being in a wheelchair creates huge opportunities to witness. People are intrigued by my story and then seem to open up more than they would to an able-bodied person. God has used my disability to open hearts to the gospel. I found this more so with indigenous Bantu-speaking patients, who had been isolated by Apartheid in South Africa.

Of course during the years post-accident there were many people who prayed for my physical healing, including my own father. I appreciated his theology, which said, 'God, please may Barry be healed, but not my will, but your will be done.' To this day I do not refuse someone who feels led to pray for my healing, but I, like Paul, have learned to be content with whatever the situation. If God, in his infinite wisdom, sees fit to leave me in a wheelchair for some reason, that is fine by me. I know he can heal me, but I know he must have a good reason why he has not chosen to do it yet. I have often said, 'If my disability is used by God to bring just one person to Christ and to rescue that person from hell, then it is totally worth it.' I can also more easily reach fellow disabled people with the good news of Jesus than an able-bodied person can. Although all disabilities vary greatly, at least disabled people can relate more easily to others who have had similar problems. My worth or joy in life does not come from being physically fit and well; it comes from the fact that I am a person loved by God. God's love is also unconditional, which I have mentioned before, and not dependent on whether I can walk or not. At church I heard Jackie Pullinger speak on her mission experience of working with drug addicts in the walled city in Hong Kong. She inspired me by saying that God uses the weak things in the world to shame the wise. She encouraged people to step out in faith, if we believe God had called us to missions.

## Our Call to Cross-Cultural Missions

As time passed I began to feel a growing call to be involved in mission work. I found it so fulfilling talking to people about the Lord. It was as if I had rivers of water inside me that needed to flow out to others. Jesus said to the woman at the well in John 4:14, 'Indeed, the water I give them will become in them a spring of water welling up to eternal life.' I felt compelled to share the good news of Jesus, and began to be drawn more to indigenous Bantu-speaking people in South Africa, because they seemed to be hungry for Jesus and God's word. As I thought of my future, the idea of working in a lucrative middle-class practice, doing expensive dental procedures and making lots of money, no longer appealed to me. I could sense that the wealthier people I talked to about the Lord were not really interested. Often they would say, 'Oh, I have tried that, but it did not work for me.' Some would say, 'I have heard it all before, and I am not interested.' Oswald J. Smith's words, 'Why should anyone hear the gospel twice, before everyone has heard it once?' really resonated with me.[2]

In my fourth year of dental studies while leading a Campus Crusade for Christ training evening of about sixty students, I met Julia. I experienced a 'love at first sight' moment and I do believe God had been preparing her for me, to become my soul mate and my partner in the gospel. After about three months of dating her I asked her a veiled question: 'Would you consider marrying an evangelist?' To my amazement she said, 'Yes, if the evangelist is you.' I told her that I was not planning on becoming a wealthy dentist, but rather to serve God full-time as an evangelist. She said that from the time she became a believer, God had given her a heart for missions, and a desire to reach lost souls. We thought, as she was studying nursing, and myself dentistry, that we could do medical missions. We could perhaps use our medical skills to get into countries that were closed to Christianity. We were more and more inspired by biographies of missionaries, including Albert Schweitzer and David Livingstone; and finally by Don Richardson's book, *Peace Child*, which encouraged us to think about the need for cultural relevance and language to reach unreached people.

I had hours of discussion with my dad, who could not understand why I wanted to become a missionary in a distant land, or in some jungle in central Africa in a wheelchair, when I could effectively witness to my dental patients in South Africa. He would also argue that I could rather use all the money I was earning to send others to the mission field. I could not see myself living in suburbia, working eight or ten hours a day fixing teeth, and paying off a huge loan to buy all the equipment needed for a dental surgery. After all, teeth will one day end up in a bucket after being extracted, or will rot in the grave. I felt I would rather spend my working hours ministering to the never-dying soul of a person. Jesus' words about the inestimable value he places on a human soul really spoke to me. Matthew 16:26 says, 'What good will it be for someone to gain the whole world, yet forfeit their soul? Or what can anyone give in exchange for their soul?'

We heard about Africa School of Missions, which offered a three-year course for people with medical skills to reach the unreached. The college was in a rural, economically deprived 'homeland' area, where one could learn on the job and get great experience before going to the field. It seemed the perfect place for us and we applied to do a three-year residential missionary training course.

We enrolled in its School of Health, but after three months felt clearly led by the Lord to join the School of Bible Translation. People do need good health and strong teeth, but we sensed our passion was rather to give them a lasting gift, the eternal word of God, which will never pass away. It is God's word that transforms people, just as it had transformed our lives. When God spoke to me about his calling on my life, he pointed me to 2 Timothy 3:16–17. God's word needed to be central in the work of discipling and equipping others.

## Disability at Work on the Mission Field

Over the three years at mission college, Julia and I decided to spend our Sundays going into the neighbouring homeland, which was at that time called Kangwane. We learned a few Siswati phrases to be able to greet the people and share a brief gospel message. The services were very long and tiring. The roads were all dust roads and the churches were generally not very accessible. There was still rioting and unrest from Apartheid, and people had only recently been burned to death with the famous car tyre necklacing. White people were considered enemies of the blacks in South Africa, but here again, I believe my being in a wheelchair was a tool of reconciliation which God used. I came in my weakness and disability to bring a message of God's love, and we were never threatened or disturbed. It showed me that I could cope in rural areas in my wheelchair. If it was raining, mud would stick to my wheels and my hands seemed always dirty. It was always a great relief to get to my basin at home to wash my hands and face in the luxury of running water, which they did not have. They also only had pit toilets, which were impossible to get into with my wheelchair, so I would have to time my liquid intake and toilet stops carefully.

After I graduated I joined the Word for the World Bible Translators. The leadership have always been very supportive and positive about my being in a wheelchair, and not seen it as a problem. Perhaps they could see that I was positive and handling my disability well. In fact I was the first missionary in the organization who went to live in a foreign country. That country was Malawi. We went to complete a Bible translation project for the Sena people. Our mission has a policy that the local church at home should be involved in sending their missionaries out, which our pastor was happy to do. On our first exploratory trip to Malawi as missionaries, our old car broke down a few times. One time it broke down near a missionary's house whom we were going to visit in a remote area. He helped us fix the car, but a comment he made was very hurtful, as he evaluated my being a missionary in a wheelchair. He said to me, 'It takes two thirds of the navy to keep one third afloat. I strongly advise you that it would be too difficult for you to live in a third world setting. You should rather stay at home and work as a dentist and send the money you make to the field to support missionaries.' This type of comment had also been made by many of my family and friends.

I had a clear sense of call and so did Julia. Perhaps these comments made us even more determined to fulfil God's call on our lives, and prove them wrong: God can and does use disabled people to fulfil his purpose.

The final breakdown of our old car occurred on our way home from Malawi, which was a 2000 kilometre trip. Our pastor at home at the time was an expert at fixing cars. He drove 1200 kms to rescue us in Zimbabwe, where our gearbox had literally shattered at the drive shaft area. He lovingly towed us and our car back to Benoni, found a second-hand gearbox and fitted it in for us. He saw our determination and proceeded to start a car fund, and the church raised enough money for me to purchase a brand new robust vehicle. The pastor jokingly said, 'I am determined not to have to drive so far to rescue you again.' I have experienced unbelievable love and compassion as people see my determination to accomplish God's will and calling for my life.

In fact our deputation to raise support around the churches in South Africa was very successful and we have been well supported by churches and individuals. Many of them remembered me through our family crisis when I had my accident almost ten years before. It also helped that they knew my dad was a pastor, but I believe it was the wheelchair that really connected us. People like a story of overcoming the odds. Here I give all the glory to God for helping me to overcome my disability.

The Sena people of Malawi are an extremely poor people group, and 99 percent of them live without running water and flushing toilets. Several people tried to dissuade us from going to Malawi as missionaries due to my disability. We realized it would not be possible to live in the very isolated and under-developed Sena area due to my physical limitations, so we lived in Blantyre, the nearest city to the Sena. God provided a comfortable home, where we worked in an office in the backyard.

The Word for the World's approach to Bible translation is that we train and assist mother-tongue speakers to translate the Bible for their own people. We do not learn the language and become experts in its grammar: we see the translators as the experts of their own language. We trained three mother-tongue Sena speakers in principles of translation and exegesis, and helped to check the accuracy of their translation against the original languages of Greek and Hebrew. We completed the entire Bible in a record ten years. Maybe being a wheelchair user meant that I was less easily distracted from the task!

We visited the Sena area several times a year to train reviewers and work with them to ensure acceptability and naturalness of the translation. The Sena Bible was published by Bible Society of Malawi in 2006. Bible translation is an ideal ministry for people with physical limitations, as a lot of time is spent working with computers and teaching and mentoring the translators. It is a privilege to spend so much time in the Scriptures, as well as to ensure that the translation is accurate, clear and natural in the receptor language. It is not a physically demanding job, but more academically challenging. Field-testing, working with reviewer committees and Bible distribution can be covered by other members of the team (though I did spend much time doing this). I personally went to distribute 30,000 gospels to 72 schools in the Sena area and loved the adventure of driving in four-wheel-drive country in my two-wheel-drive car.

During our ten-year stay in Malawi, Julia and I raised two lovely adopted children, Lisa and Timothy. A book called *Operation Jonah* (by Elisabeth Miller) tells of the amazing community involvement in the recovery of Timothy, who was kidnapped from our home in Blantyre when he was fourteen months old.[3] Once again I believe it was due to my disability that people rallied to help us to find our son, who was missing for three days. They sensed our vulnerability and need, and with God's prompting, over seventy people were involved in the search operation.

After completing the work on the Sena Bible, God called us to go to Tanzania, but I was advised to return to South Africa for serious medical attention. After more than twenty bouts of malaria, my kidneys were damaged. I had night sweats and fevers for the last five years in Malawi. The doctors decided that my bladder should be removed and a urostomy be done. I was told I should also not return to a malaria area. After much prayer, and the bold faith of my dad, we decided to trust God for healing. By God's grace my kidney function improved greatly and I did not have the surgery. Within nine months I was back to full health.

God blessed us to adopt a third child, Daniel, in South Africa, and when he was eight months old, we drove 4000 km to Tanzania as a family in our hand-controlled four wheel drive vehicle with all our possessions in a big trailer. God has certainly given me a can-do attitude and our mission generally gives us freedom to put our faith into action, and do what we feel led to do. God had given me a vision to be involved in twenty Bible translation projects in Tanzania, a country with 130 languages, and more than one hundred needing a translation of the Bible. A person from another Bible agency in South Africa actually laughed at me when I told him this. He said, 'We are scaling down, and no society should take on more than eight projects.' I told him of The Word for the World's training program, which enables us to start many projects at one time. William Carey said, 'Expect great things from God and attempt great things for God.'[4] Hebrews 11:6 says that without faith it is impossible to please God.

By God's grace we were able to start ten Bible translation projects within two years of being in Tanzania, and all ten had their New Testaments published in 2016. A further five translation projects were started just after we handed the work over to a national leader whom I had trained to take over from me. Our five years in Tanzania were very productive and, as

I had obtained an MA degree in sociolinguistics from the University of South Africa (UNISA) via correspondence, I was asked to become a Bible Translation consultant, mainly in South East Asia and Africa. I trained up a team of nationals to take over all of my responsibilities in our ethos of empowering nationals.

From Tanzania we moved to England in 2009, as I was asked to develop the UK as a support base for our work. I could also travel freely from the UK for my consultancy. In order to empower nationals, I realized that my role needed to change to being more of a trainer and fundraiser, to grow our capacity on the field. Although I had contracted malaria a further five times in Tanzania, my general health was good. God truly sustained me. I try to be physically active and play sport to keep fit. I swim about twice a week and play golf from my wheelchair once a week. I took up sailing too.

My calling to the field with its potential health problems due to tropical diseases is still strong. I believe that my disability has taught me to depend on God for everything. I rely on him to help me to get around. This can mean receiving help from others to go upstairs, or getting medical attention in developing world hospitals. Or it can mean waiting for another bus because the hoist to get a wheelchair onto the first bus is not working; or asking for assistance to my plane seat on an aisle wheelchair. This dependency on God has also enabled me to trust him in difficult and life-threatening journeys for the sake of his kingdom. As Paul says in Philippians 1:21, 'For to me, to live is Christ and to die is gain.' I do not fear death.

In August 2011, after being in the UK for two years, I took on a fundraising challenge to hand-cycle 1600 km from Land's End in the south to John o'Groats in the north, which we named *Wheels for the Word*. I completed the journey in twenty-three days, and spoke in churches along the way, raising £25,000 for Bible translation. The trip was a testimony to how God had healed my kidneys ten years earlier, and sustained me after being wheelchair-bound for nearly thirty years.

I currently travel to South East Asia and Africa up to ten times per year and have checked over fifty different languages as a consultant. A big challenge is getting up and down stairs in buildings which do not have lifts, and on almost every visit I have to be carried up and down two flights of steps on a daily basis. In South East Asia I need a very narrow wheelchair, so that I can get through the narrow bathroom doors. The people are extremely friendly and willing to help in this. This dependence on them shows my weakness and vulnerability, and I believe it is a way of bonding with them. I help them, but they also help me.

In Tanzania we pioneered with our team the concept of *group consultant checking* where I can check up to ten languages at once in a consultation. With computer technology one can look at up to ten English back translations of a verse at a time and discuss any translation problems, or areas that need correcting, all in one sitting. This method has helped to save time and money and results in good quality translations as the knowledge of a crowd is better than the knowledge of one expert. The teams learn so much from each other when they get together. This approach of group checking has been implemented by many other Bible agencies.

## Conclusion

I can honestly say that my disability has not in any way been a stumbling block to missions; it has served rather as a springboard. God has used me to make great strides in the world of Bible translation through my disability. I believe that through my near-death experience and resulting paraplegia God has given me a second chance to serve him. This has also created in me a sense of urgency, in that time is a short and precious commodity. All human beings are only one last breath away from eternity. My disability has taught me how insignificant working legs are in the light of souls and their eternal wellbeing.

This sense of urgency, and the huge need to get the Bible translated into all remaining languages in order to reach the lost, caused me to think innovatively as to how we can speed up Bible translation without sacrificing quality. How do Bible-less people groups get through trauma and disability without God's word to feed them and build them up? I can't imagine what it would have been like for me without God's word in those early months after my accident and even today, as I read it daily.

During one of my training sessions recently in South East Asia a student made the following remark: 'If Barry can come here and teach us in this heat (it was 47°C), and battle as he does in his wheelchair, never complaining as he is carried up and down steps, then I want to give my all to translate the Bible into my language.' Actions do speak louder than words. God has used my disability to inspire and encourage others.

Mission agencies should realise that not sending a person as a missionary because of their disability could well be short-changing the people group who need them, because Christ's strength is made perfect in our weakness (2 Corinthians 12:9). 'How beautiful are the wheels of those who bring Good News' (a paraplegic adaptation of Romans 10:15).

## *Acknowledgements*

I would not have been able to do cross-cultural missions without my long-suffering and beautiful wife, Julia, who so often has been a physical and spiritual help to me. I am grateful to The Word for the World Bible Translators, who never saw my disability as a reason for me not to be involved in frontline missions.

CHAPTER 6

# Paul the Leper and Olive the Servant

David C Deuel
Joni and Friends Christian Institute on Disability
United States

As the stories in this book make clear, God's people have infinite value, regardless of whether they accomplish great works. They *are* his great works. This is supported by biblical argument. There is an important place for those who are weak, whom God gifts uniquely, and whom he uses to accomplish his mighty deeds. Many people with disabling conditions are called and gifted to be leaders, and their weakness can become God's platform to bring glory to himself. No one accomplishes great works for God unless God enables his children in their weakness. The story of Olive Doke and Paul Kasonga demonstrates further what the weakest of the weak can do with God's enabling.

## Olive Doke's Early Life as a Missionary

The story of Olive Doke, a missionary sent out through the South African Baptist Missionary Society (SABMS), and her student Kaputula Kasonga, a Zambian national who developed leprosy, is buried treasure in the history of missions. Their testimony reveals a special kind of ministry relationship in God's theatre of weakness. From his youth, Kaputula had multiple severe and worsening disabilities that came with leprosy, including difficulty in walking, chronic pain, inability to write and recurrent illnesses. What the Lord accomplished through him during his brief life is amazing by any standard. But the story is only half told if we neglect the role of Olive Doke. She did more than encourage and advocate; in addition to ministering to the young women in Zambia, the work for which she was sent out, she facilitated Kaputula's work. In every case we know of, she respected his dignity.

Olive and Kaputula's story begins with Baptist missionaries Henry Masters and Arthur Philips, who planted the Kafulafuta mission in 1905, in what was then known as Lambaland, in former Northern Rhodesia. Masters explained their plan: 'Africa can never be evangelized by the direct effort of the missionary alone. After the pioneering has been done, it is for the missionary to train, inspire, and organize a staff of local evangelists.'[1]

Olive Doke was born in Bristol, England, to a family passionate about missions. The Doke family moved to South Africa when Olive was very young. In 1916, at the age of twenty-five, Olive left the comforts of her home in Johannesburg to serve at the Kafulafuta mission, far out in the Zambian jungle. Olive describes the state of the mission's work when she arrived:

> The work was still in the pioneer stages, and a great deal of 'trekking' had to be done, involving long journeys of hundreds of miles on foot through African forest infested by wild animals of every description. It was still the days of primitive travel with native porters carrying the necessary camp equipment and barter goods. One had to depend on one's rifle to secure meat for the pot, as well as to buy meal for the carriers. The country inhabited by the Lamba tribe extended over 30,000 square miles of forest—and this was our parish.[2]

The Kafulafuta mission already had a boarding school for boys. Within a decade, Olive opened a boarding school for girls, a ministry passion that continued throughout her time there. But God had plans for Olive that went far beyond her own vision for the work at Kafulafuta.

## Kaputula 'Paul' Kasonga's Conversion and Training

Kaputula Kasonga was around fourteen when he arrived at the boys' school. Precociously bright, he listened attentively as Miss Doke explained the gospel in her Bible lessons. Kaputula says:

> I was then a schoolboy and heard the word of God. . . . The words of a hymn we sang, 'Jesus is coming again' arrested me and made me think, so I went to Shikulu Doke [Olive's brother, Clement], who also served at the school, and that night had a talk with him, and there and then gave my heart to the Lord.[3]

When school let out for the holidays, the children returned to their homes, with the expectation that they would return once school was back in session. But Kaputula did not return and no one knew what had happened to him. Months passed by.

Standard practice at the mission was that teams of missionaries would go out 'trekking' into the villages to find places where the gospel had not been preached. Upon arrival, the missionaries would ask the villagers if they had heard about Jesus. The response was often that they had not. One day, a team entered a new area and posed the question. The response was that the people of that village had indeed heard the gospel. When asked how they had heard, their response was that Kaputula had told them. After more inquiring they discovered that Kaputula had contracted leprosy and lived across the river in a hut. Olive explains: 'Food and water was taken to him there, but he was by himself, an outcast, unclean! He had been faithful in witness and now was cast-out! This was his first great lesson. "Have faith in God."'[4] The missionaries took him back to the mission to care for him and with medication they stabilized the leprosy so that he was able to return to school.

When Lambas—the people of that region—came to Christ, they changed their names to Bible names. At his baptism, Kaputula changed his name to Paul, the apostle of weakness, who also had an infirmity. Olive tells the story of baptismal renaming: 'How prophetic was this name of Paul to be! A man with a thorn in the flesh! And what a thorn! Leprosy! He too proved that the grace of the Lord Jesus was sufficient for him, his strength was indeed made perfect in weakness.'[5] Even Kaputula's new name, Paul, reminded all who knew him of his weakness. Paul was the first national to be baptized at the mission, and his weakness associated with his leprosy shaped the mission and its witness to the surrounding villages, and out to distant areas.

## Producing Materials for Ministry

Paul's ability to read and write made him stand out. As his committed teacher, Olive describes Paul in school: 'So Kaputula continued his schooling. In school he did well. He was easily top boy. Then he became a pupil teacher, but, best of all, his example of Christian living told on his companions and, one by one, they too came out for Jesus.'[6] In spite of the challenges presented by his illness and disabilities, Paul demonstrated his gift and calling as a very young man. The Lord's blessing on Paul gave his beloved leaders who trained him confidence to take him along when they launched a new school in Kawunda Chiwele. Paul tells the story:

> Shikulu Doke and Walona Doke went with me and Mose Katanga to open the school. They left us there while they went off itinerating in the villages. Whilst there, Mose and I constantly preached the word of God in the surrounding villages, and quite a number responded to the message and became hearers.[7]

As his advisors entrusted Paul with gospel treasure, Paul accepted these opportunities with both zeal and a measure of caution. His passion to serve carefully was guided by his study of God's word.

Olive taught Paul to love Scripture, an attribute that he nurtured and never lost. It was the passion that fueled his skill in handling Scripture like a noble Berean. With a keen intellect, Paul was able to read carefully and interpret the Bible faithfully. This commitment was perhaps facilitated by the time granted him due to the lack of mobility caused by his disability. Paul's ability with language made him a highly qualified candidate for working on literacy projects of all sorts, one example of which was his ministering through writing letters, in which he emulated the apostle whose name he bore. In short, the Bible was the fountain of Paul's ministry and the impetus for all of Paul's work in missions.

Because Paul knew the various shades of meaning behind the Lamba words, he was able to assist Olive and the missionaries to find the right words as they translated various biblical texts and other books from English into Lamba.[8] They worked at meeting the great need for a Bible and study tools. They understood, in the words of Conrad Mbewe, 'the need to learn the language of the indigenous people, reduce it to written communication, teach the indigenous people how to read and write, [and] translate the Bible and other relevant books into the language of the indigenous people.'[9] Olive helped in the translation of the first Lamba Bible and wrote many readers, primers and other educational and religious materials in Lamba. Paul helped in many of these projects and contributed in particular to the Bible translation into the Lamba language.

Paul Kasonga was also a gifted preacher and leader. Paul preached from his weakness and in God's power. Some of the Lambas believed that Paul's greatest gift was his preaching. He became 'the very first local leader of the Baptist church in Zambia. . . . He was the first local person to whom the missionaries first gave actual leadership and authority.'[10] Although the date is uncertain, this probably occurred in 1931. In 1934, Anasi Lupunga joined Paul as his assistant at the Kafulafuta mission, until Paul's death twenty years later.

## Evangelizing and Shepherding

At about eighteen years of age, Paul was offered a teaching role at a remote area that could only be reached on foot, even though he could hardly walk. He accepted the invitation and became a trusted teacher for a white settlement owner who had multiple wives and six children, all of whom became Paul's students in one way or another. Here again, Paul used his time off to go out into the villages and preach the gospel. When he returned to the mission, he learned the trade of carpentry but continued to go out to villages to preach the gospel, sometimes with his colleagues, other times alone. Regardless of whatever else he needed to do, this became his common practice. He had to preach Christ to his countrymen.

*Rev Paul Kasonga with Rev Bob Litana and Rev Anasi Lupunga. (Used with permission of Pastor Mark Penrith, archivist of the Baptist Union of South Africa.)*

Paul's knowledge of Scripture and his giftedness for preaching and teaching might easily eclipse his gift for counselling others, particularly those in conflict. His own brokenness in disability became fertile soil for the roots of a compassionate, understanding and humble counselor, such as he became. His preaching and teaching was accompanied by strong and effective relationships with church people, and this could be seen in their family lives and their marriages. His commitment to his people and the way he labored among them was almost incomprehensible. People would line up at his doorway to listen to his advice, and he would sit with his Bible resting on a makeshift tray fastened to the chair in front of him. "At any time of the day and night almost, enquirers would be found in his hut, with him pointing them the way of salvation, or strengthening, advising and guiding them in their spiritual life, showing them how it all fitted in with their daily round in the village."[11]

One by one, he addressed their needs from Scripture and sent them on their way better equipped. Olive captures the impact of Paul's counselling:

> He, with his wisdom, was instrumental in saving many marriages which would have come to divorce. Those who were determined to separate, after long conversation and prayer with Paul, have gone away in a different frame of mind, and, with God's help have kept together.[12]

Paul Kasonga never married and had no children, but he had a deep grasp of Scripture's teaching about marriage. So, as Olive adds regarding those whom Paul counseled, 'They are with us today as happy families, living witnesses to Paul's loving tenderness and understanding, and yet persistence, in maintaining God's laws about marriage.'[13]

As time went on, Paul's mobility became limited and his travel decreased. He began an extensive letter-writing ministry, following in the path of his namesake, the apostle Paul. 'Where he could not go physically, he went through his letters. Elison Chimbila, who was a deacon in the church at Kafulafuta, became his scribe because Kasanga could not write very well, having lost his fingers.'[14] From his own pain, Paul spoke to the hearts of his people through correspondence. Mbewe adds, 'Kasanga wrote letters of encouragement or admonition or guidance and comfort to various churches, and to various individuals in those churches who needed help right across Lambaland. It is a wonder how much God did through his servant *despite* his infirmity.'[15] Alternatively, perhaps *because of* his infirmity and immobility, he had the time to commit to composing powerful pastoral letters that encouraged and guided the growing church in Zambia . . . very much like the apostle Paul.

Clearly, Paul Kasonga's disabilities shaped him into an outstanding, and yet humble, pastor. He lost all his fingers and toes and eventually a lower leg. He was chronically ill. At the time he was ordained, he could neither walk nor write without assistance. Most of the time, he was restricted to his house like the apostle, whose hired house in Rome became a centre for

Christian mission (Acts 28:30–31).[16] For any travel, he relied on others to transport him on a stretcher. Yet others valued his giftedness, commitment and spiritual insight. This dependence on others, due to disability, was part of his *ability* to build a healthy church. It created a healthy interdependence. Yet another example of God reframing disability as ability!

Paul's suffering, often severe, gave him a rapport with the suffering poor, sick and outcast. He understood their pain, responded with empathy, and was slow to judge people in their struggles. He cared deeply for those who were infirm and weak. In his own weakness he ministered to their needs as well as he possibly could. The impact of his kindness in weakness was seen and heard across Lambaland. Olive explains that Paul and his assistant pastor were 'ever helping the weaker and more backward, and zealously watching over the purity of the church membership. It is their individual work which tells perhaps more than anything.'[17]

Through Paul, his people understood and accepted their need to draw upon weakness. 'If a man in his condition could do so much, how much more should those of us who are able-bodied do?'[18] Olive describes the impact of Paul's ministry:

> It soon became evident that Paul was a born leader; the people seemed naturally to look to him. He was far ahead of them in spiritual things; he had been taught of the Holy Spirit by his very suffering. . . . Paul soon became the acknowledged leader in Lambaland in spiritual things, and everybody naturally went to him with troubles and difficulties.[19]

Zambian church planter Conrad Mbewe's conclusion is that all believers 'ought to read the life of Paul Kasonga and put aside their excuses for not serving God because of their alleged inabilities.'[20] Perhaps hidden to the casual observer, Paul's disabilities gave him ministry integrity among his peers and valuable spiritual insight for preaching and counselling. The church today needs pastors, missionaries, Sunday school teachers and other leaders with disabilities. Perhaps ironically, it suffers spiritually without them. Their weakness, like Paul Kasonga's, should be cherished.

## Completing Their Mission

Within ten years of beginning his ministry, Paul was at the top level of leadership at the Kafulafuta church, but it took another twenty-two years before he was ordained. Paul was selected to be the first national elder of the church and was ordained to the gospel ministry a little over one year before the Lord took him home.[21]

*Taken just days before Paul's death, this photo shows him studying the Scriptures. (Used with permission of Pastor Mark Penrith, archivist of the Baptist Union of South Africa.)*

At around age fifty, Paul's leprosy took its toll. Olive wrote,

> Paul the Leper has finished his course. The earth of Lambaland has received his mortal remains, so marked by suffering. The rivers flow past his grave on either side, trees and palms lining their banks. In weakness of body he had 'fought a good fight' and in the midst of Central African heathenism he had 'kept the faith.' His is the 'crown of righteousness,' a mighty tribute to the grace of God.[22]

Olive served almost until her death in 1972, fifty-six years after going to the Kafulafuta mission. She had invested her entire life in one place, much of it working alongside one person, Paul Kasonga. In so doing, she became, and is to this day, the longest-serving Baptist missionary in the history of

Zambia. By one testimony, 'The spread of the gospel in Lambaland can be attributed mainly to the work of these two.'[23] And elsewhere, 'God used these two wonderful servants of Christ greatly in the establishment of the Baptist churches in Zambia. They were both pioneers and pillars of the work there.'[24] Today, the record of their service for Christ reminds us timelessly that God's strength is perfected in our disability, in weakness.

CHAPTER 7

# Being a Mission Partner with Disability in Kenya

Paul Lindoewood
United Kingdom

## Introduction

I am a wheelchair user with limited dexterity and with communication impairments, both hearing and speech. I have always required assistance with daily activities, and this is now provided through a group of helpers (Personal Assistants—PAs) whom I employ. Nobody really knows how I became the way I am. Mine was apparently a breech birth, and one month premature. I was born at home and hospitalised straight away, and put in an incubator, as I was found to be jaundiced. All such scenarios in 1957 would have been strong contenders for developing cerebral palsy.

This question, though, has never concerned me. People are fat or slim, tall or short—why should I not be as I am, as God has made me?

I appreciate that this may not be the experience of every person with a disability. Some conditions are accompanied by severe physical pain, increasing levels of impairment, or long periods in a hospital. I have been blessed by a relatively pain-free life, although, as I get older, my joints and muscles do start to complain. However, by far the biggest issues I have faced as a person with a disability relate to how people react to my existence, rather than a feeling of bereavement over what I can and cannot do.

Much of my life has been spent managing a conflict between how I see my own situation and how other people perceive it. For example, the very idea of someone like me, with all my disabilities, being involved in mission in rural Kenya would have been beyond most people's expectations. For many people, including colleagues with disability, the idea of my living and working in rural Africa was incomprehensible and even 'threatening.' For me it was primarily a question of whether the practical issues could be overcome. Perhaps this apparently rebellious self-image stemmed from my teenage years, when I expected to have a career and get married and so on. I rarely saw my disability as a reason not to expect this.

I did not discover the biblical truths confirming my self-perception until I reached my twenties and thirties. Then I looked closely at: (1) the fact that 'God created mankind in his own image' (Genesis 1:27); (2) the person of Moses in the Exodus story; (3) Isaiah's prophesy, often said to be describing Jesus. 'He grew up before him like a tender shoot, and like a root out of dry ground. He had no beauty or majesty to attract us to him, nothing in his appearance that we should desire him' (53:2); and (4) the idea of the church being a body that is made up of many parts in 1 Corinthians 12. Verse 22 develops the idea of supporting those who are deemed to be weaker, as they are indispensable.

## *Being Different*

Many experiences heightened my awareness that, despite efforts to get on with life in the same way as anyone else, I was regarded as different. I think, for example, of a Saturday afternoon when I and a group of teenage friends with disabilities from my special school were completing our Duke of Edinburgh Bronze Award expedition. When we returned, we discovered that the Head Teacher had received two phone calls from people in the nearby village, asking whether four of his pupils had 'escaped.' Or of an incident in my early twenties, while I was doing a short course at St. John's Theological College in Nottingham: A fellow student who happened to be with me in the common room one day was clearly embarrassed at the idea of leaving me on my own. She asked who was responsible for looking after me. I had to reply 'nobody'!

To think of people like me serving in mission in rural Africa required a large shift of mind-set. I thank God for enabling this to happen, which is clearer to see now with hindsight.

## *My Early Years*

My first experience of Africa was in 1958, when my family went to live in Lagos, Nigeria. This was because my father's employers needed someone to develop their business in West Africa. We came home when I was five years old and I was educated through the special school system of the 1960s and '70s. My interest in Africa was kept alive by my father's continued work throughout what is now called Sub-Saharan Africa.

After completing my degree in Public Administration at Trent Polytecnic (1983), I had a number of jobs within the British Disability and Independent Living Movement. Between 1994 and '96, I completed a master's in disability studies. I also became active within the World Development Movement, currently called Global Justice Now, and from 1991–1995 was a Liberal Democrat Town Councillor.

## *Independent Living*

The most significant development in terms of inclusion into everyday life came in November 1981, as a student at Trent Poly. I moved into my own flat with the support of Personal Assistants who, at that time, were provided through Community Service Volunteers (CSV). The system through which PAs are provided has changed over the decades, but the fundamental principle remains that for many persons with a physical and/or sensory disability, their need is for a pair of arms and legs or ears or eyes, not 'a carer.' The debate around this assertion raged particularly fiercely during the '80s and still continues. It heavily influenced my understanding of Independent Living.

Nowadays, in Britain, many people with disabilities use a system called Direct Payments, through which their local council provides the money to enable them to employ their own PAs. This has allowed me to recruit local personnel in India and the USA, as well as in the UK. As part of the enablement package for my work in Kenya, the Methodist Church paid for me to have two PAs, thereby continuing this principle. I have often reflected on how God used my struggle to develop mechanisms for independent living as a training ground for my future work in mission.

## *Developing a Christian Faith*

It was during my teenage years that I started to become interested in Christianity as a living faith. I don't know exactly when I crossed the line into faith but remember a growing conviction in the teachings of Jesus and an acceptance that he was God in human form.

Over the years and decades, my Christian faith has moved from acknowledging the person of Jesus to accepting him as a personal Saviour, and looking at important issues through a biblical lens. Our Christian mission cannot be understood only in terms of personal salvation, although this is a crucial part of the overall picture. In Romans 8:18–22 we read how our mission is to liberate creation itself. This awareness has increasingly led me to look at social justice and environmental issues as part of my Christian discipleship. Due to my background, it was natural that my focus should home in on the needs of people with a disability and their families.

## Disability and the Christian Church

The church can be a difficult place for people with disability, particularly if they are new to the faith. The church often emphasises Jesus as the man who made the lame walk, made the deaf hear and gave sight to the blind (Luke 7:22). Whilst this is true, and should not be diminished, it does not mean that the purpose in life of people with disability is to be fodder for miracles.

The Bible also teaches that God made human beings 'in his own image' (Genesis 1:27) and, of course, we are all 'fearfully and wonderfully made' (Psalm 139:14). There are no qualifications to this like having 'normal physical, sensory or cognitive functions.' There is no need for us to see ourselves as sub-human because we have impairments. The church does not always seem to recognize this, perhaps because of wider cultural influence. In my earlier years as a Christian I could be heard saying, 'I never question my Christian faith because of the way I am. But I do sometimes question it because of the way some Christians respond to the way I am.'

So long as churches acknowledge the presence of people with disability only as those to be cared for, and overlook their contribution, they are not likely to promote their presence in mission. How many people know about servants of God who had a disability, such as Ian Stillman, who worked with deaf people by developing the Nambiikkai project in India? How many had heard about Paul Kaputula Kasonga and his work to establish the Evangelical Church in Zambia? In the 2015 video on Youtube, 'Bad Legs,' Elinor Young, who experienced polio when she was five, describes the embarrassment of fellow church members when she went up to the front, after a call from the speaker, to say she was available for God's mission.[1] Apparently, someone even apologised to the speaker that the only person to respond to his call was 'a cripple' who clearly could not be expected to do anything! That was in the 1950s. Similar attitudes prevailed in the 1980s and 1990s, and perhaps still do today. Elinor spent many years working with the people of Papua, Indonesia.

### *God the Enabler*

What could be called a 'care only' mind-set has a strong influence on people with disabilities and on those around them. In many situations this mind-set is not only unnecessary, but unbiblical.

We frequently talk about God as our 'enabler' and that is certainly true within the mission context. The verb 'to enable' is the opposite of the verb 'to disable,' and both can be applied to anyone, whether or not they have an impairment. Discussions around the inclusion of people with disability in mission will often come down to whether the church or mission agency can resource the enablement package. In my situation, this amounted to paying for two PAs, a vehicle that I could access, and the building of paths to allow me to get to my house in the hospital compound.

Consider Moses' response to God, in Exodus 4:10, to excuse him from having to go to Pharaoh: 'Pardon your servant, Lord. I have never been eloquent, neither in the past nor since you have spoken to your servant. I am slow of speech and tongue.' It comes over as a reasonable excuse by the world's standards. Although the exact nature of Moses' speech issue is unclear I can draw parallels to my experience with speech difficulties. In my case, I could have said: 'There are so many things that I cannot do independently, such as dressing and bathing. The everyday environment is hardly going to be wheelchair friendly. I have a speech impairment that makes it very difficult for some people to understand me, even if they speak English. I am also legally regarded in the UK as "a vulnerable person." How could I possibly be suited for mission in rural Kenya?' God replies to Moses, as he does to me, saying: 'Who gave human beings their mouths? Who makes them deaf or mute? Who gives them sight or makes them blind? Is it not I, the Lord?' (Exodus 4:11). The discussion continues and in verses 14–16 God says to Moses:

> What about your brother, Aaron the Levite? I know he can speak well. He is already on his way to meet you, and he will be glad to see you. You shall speak to him and put words in his mouth; I will help both of you speak and will teach you what to do. He will speak to the people for you, and it will be as if he were your mouth and as if you were God to him.

This parallels the role of my helpers in enabling my mission work.

It was a revelation when, in the mid-1980s, the curate of my then church highlighted that Moses had an issue with speaking. We do not know if this represented a formal speech impairment; however, it justified a second person assisting him. The idea that Moses successfully negotiated the Israelites' freedom, and then led them for forty years in the wilderness, despite this, was not beyond reason to me. We should note that Aaron was an enabler, and not a carer.

Please understand, I am not saying that people with disability should not be cared for. Everyone needs that—whether they're disabled or not. If God had approached Moses' slowness of speech and heavy tongue with the 'care only' mind-set, the Jews' exodus from Egypt might have been a different story. Likewise, if the Methodist Church had adopted a 'care only' mind-set, my mission work in Kenya would have been a non-starter.

## My Interest in Mission and Development Work

During the 1980s and '90s, I became aware that I was living within social structures that dictated how services and support systems were provided. These created a culture that appeared to perpetuate a 'care only' response. Care services played an important role in enabling many people with disability to survive, but this culture frequently seemed to suffocate the desires and aspirations of myself and colleagues within the disability movement. One reason for my interest in working in mission and international development was to see whether we could nurture a disability-enabling context and culture if we started from a situation where there was nothing, or very little, in the way of disability services.

### *Voluntary Service Overseas*

My first attempt to work internationally came when I applied to VSO in 1989. My application was turned down on medical grounds, with a letter from the medical adviser. VSO apparently works in situations where there is little or no electricity or running water. Such contexts were deemed unsafe for someone like me.

Whilst I appreciate the assistance and comfort that such convenience can provide, particularly as I sit at my computer typing this chapter, I had not appreciated that they were a requirement for the survival of someone with cerebral palsy. People with disabilities can, and do, survive, without electricity and running water.

Since that time, VSO have made substantial advances in the inclusion of people with disability. If I made the same application now, I would receive a more constructive response. I share this story not to criticise VSO, but to show how a 'care only' agenda can frustrate, and even disable, the participation of people with disability in public life or mission.

## *The Methodist Church*

I come from an Anglican background. My contact with the Methodist Church developed through my wife, Rachel. Rachel had a strong family connection with the Methodist Church and had established a good relationship with people in its Mission Department. I started to join her at Methodist Church and World Mission events. Rachel had never hidden her long-term interest in being a mission partner and we were able to get to know key members of the Methodist Church Overseas Division.

In 1993 the Methodist Church agreed to fund me for six weeks research in Kenya. Although the research was not anything major—looking at a sample of agencies and their relationships with people with disability—the trip allowed me to show that I could manage within the East African context. With hindsight, it was an important building block towards our acceptance in 1994 as mission partners.

As we went through the application process, Rachel and I became more convinced that this was what God was calling us to do. However, I remember a word of caution from the recruitment officer that not everyone was quite so convinced. I was aware that I was seriously testing their boundaries. However, in January 1995 we received our letter informing us that we had been accepted, and that the process would start to find a partner church interested in what we could offer. As I had already travelled to Kenya, and met the Presiding Bishop of the Methodist Church there, this was a logical place to start looking.

The Methodist Church in Kenya (MCK) had one of only two Mission Hospitals in Africa that had not been taken over by national governments. They needed mission partner doctors because they could not retain local doctors in rural settings. The church gratefully accepted Rachel, a doctor, to assist in their overstretched hospital, but was not quite sure what to make of the Disability Community Worker who came with the package!

## *Arriving in Kenya*

We finally arrived in Kenya after seven months of training at Selly Oak Colleges in Birmingham, between January and July 1996, and a three-week crash course in Swahili. During this time I also managed to complete my master's thesis in disability studies amid all the packing.

The day after our arrival, Rachel and I went to the government offices to collect our visas. Rachel got hers immediately. However, mine was refused because the officer could not conceive how I could work. Declining the compromise that I could stay in Kenya as Rachel's dependent, we rushed back to the Methodist Guest House, where we knew the Presiding Bishop was preparing to leave for a conference in Brazil the next day. He lodged an appeal the next morning and my working visa finally came through, with twelve days to spare on my visitor's one.

## Our Work in Kenya

We finally arrived at Maua Methodist Hospital. It was often referred to as 'an island' surrounded by the hustle and bustle of Maua town. It was easy to develop a mind-set that said, 'People come to us when they are ill.' This was not an approach that Rachel and I wanted to adopt. Rachel's first visit to Maua had been to conduct a community health survey near to Meru Game Park in 1988, about an hour's drive from the hospital. My interest in working with people with disability also gave me a greater community focus.

My first office was in the hospital's Community Health Department, and my brief was to establish the Methodist Church in Kenya Disability Programme. However, during the next nine years I had three roles:

1. *Researcher and consultant on behalf of Action on Disability and Development.* This British-based charity working with disabled people's organizations in Africa and Asia was considering starting a programme in Kenya. When the Director heard that I was due to go to Kenya, he asked if I was interested in carrying out a feasibility study. The Methodist Churches in Britain and Kenya welcomed the idea, not least because they had little money to fund my work. This role gave me a good understanding of the situation faced by people with disability and their organizations in Kenya.

2. *Coordinator of the Methodist Church in Kenya Disability Programme.* This was to promote the inclusion of people with disability throughout the national church. Sometimes the first step was to help a church to see that there were people with disability in the community they were serving. The strategy for this programme was to establish disability groups at the Synod level, headed by people with disability.

3. *Founder and Director of the Meru North Disability Community Centre (DCC).* Essentially, this was a Community-Based Rehabilitation (CBR)

initiative, which brought together the disability services—for example, physiotherapy, occupational therapy and education—and self-help organizations for people with disability. This enabled me to have the most contact with the grassroots' disability movement, and to consider whether services could be developed with more of an 'enabling' agenda.

Being based in the hospital meant getting around was easier for me, and I was within a supportive community. But I was not always ideally based to coordinate a national research initiative or programme. During the first five years I spent a lot of time travelling to Nairobi or other places in Kenya.

A further challenge was to come when developing the DCC. It was always meant to be a community initiative, but to start with, it was located in the hospital. It was important that it should have its own land to build premises, so it could be developed as a project in its own right, with its own management structure and identity, separate from the hospital. This led to some questioning and debate, both outside and within the hospital.

I also became a local preacher. This increased the Disability Programme's profile within the Methodist Church local circuits. I was established as a regular preacher 'on note' and so preached more widely than just on 'disability' subjects. In addition to the Disability Programme we established an annual Disability Sunday. This gave disabled people, and myself, a platform to speak to the church both nationally and locally.

Although I have a severe speech impairment, I have no problem speaking. I would say 'I don't have problems talking, or understanding what I am saying. It is other people who need help with my speech.' The basic premise remains true although, as the years go by, my energy levels are lower, and public speaking makes me more tired. I enjoyed my time as a local preacher and believe that I shared the gospel effectively.

Interestingly, my role as a local preacher was far more readily accepted in Kenya than it has been in the UK. One reason for this was my use of an interpreter, which was quite normal in Kenya, due to the nation's multiple languages. The first time I preached in Kenya, I spoke from the exodus story and afterwards the church christened me and my helper, Charles, 'Moses and Aaron.'

I recall reading one of my references before leaving for Kenya. It was by my ministerial referee and it ended with what is an important piece of advice when considering people with high-support-needs. He wrote words to the effect of 'Paul will be an expensive mission partner to support. However, if you can afford the expense, you will get your money's worth.' I have often reflected on those words. I agree, I was an expensive mission partner to support. Whether they got their money's worth is not really for me to say, but I hope so!

### *Being a Person with Disabilities in Kenya*

During my work with Action on Disability and Development (ADD), I met a group of people with disabilities in Kisumu, Western Kenya. The group was being supported by a VSO worker. Evidently, after I left, the biggest subject for discussion by the group was that they had met a *muzungu (white person) with a disability*! This narrative was to be repeated on many occasions.

In areas such as rural Africa, people can feel that disability exists only in their part of the world. That may be difficult to understand in our high-tech environment, with access to so much information. An important outcome, even now, of including people with disability in mission is to demonstrate that it is a worldwide issue.

## Three Stories

Real-life stories can be more powerful than hypothetical situations. I would like to share three stories which have a strong significance for me and my ministry in Kenya. Having a Disability Programme within the Methodist Church enabled stories that otherwise might have been lost to be noticed and recorded. My first story is from a local church.

### *1. Kobia and the New Roof Offering*

One day, the Nyambene MCK Synod Development Worker came into my office. He was very excited, having come straight from a discussion with the Chair of a Methodist Church in Athi, a small market town around an hour's drive from Maua. The story he shared had taught the church an important lesson.

The church had needed a new roof and, in good Kenyan tradition, they organised a community fundraising event—known as a *harambee*. Everyone in the church was invited, and as the Chairman read out a list of members each person had gone forward and given their *pesa kidogo* (small amount of money) or *pesa kubwa* (big amount of money).

At the end of the day, people were feeling pleased with themselves, as they heard that the money raised was enough to start work on the roof. Then a hand went up at the back of the church from someone kneeling on the floor, and a voice spoke. 'My name is Kobia and I have worshipped at this church for many years. You have totally ignored me and my participation. I too want to contribute to this project.' At that, Kobia crawled on his hands and knees to the front of the church and gave his 500 Kenyan shillings.

Kobia was not part of an educated elite, arguing for inclusion on the grounds of intellectual ability. He had probably received very limited education. However, he was determined to play a role and reckoned that his inability to walk should not hinder him. He was later to represent his church on the committee of the Meru North Disability Community Centre (DCC). I was interested and encouraged by Kobia's story, not least because I had experienced very similar exclusion myself. I used this story in my local preaching, to prove that a disabled person could go beyond what was expected of them.

## *2. Stephen and the Presiding Bishop*

A second story illustrates an intriguing difference between expectations placed on me in Kenya and in the UK. It also helped me develop my understanding of inclusion.

It was a Saturday morning, around 11 a.m., and I was planning to catch up with some work at home. Then I received a text message from Rachel telling me that an HIV/Aids awareness-raising day had just started in the local Methodist Church. The day was being chaired by the MCK Presiding Bishop and, although the subject matter did not directly affect my work, I decided to show my face.

I parked my wheelchair next to my good friend Stephen Gitonga, Manager of the Maua Hospital Palliative Care Programme. HIV/AIDS directly affected Stephen's work and it was no surprise when he was invited to say a few words about his department. His address was in the local language of Kimeru, which I didn't speak. At the very end of his speech Stephen suddenly jumped into English, saying, 'I think my good friend Paul Lindoewood would like to say a few words'! I literally had the time it takes to turn a wheelchair a hundred and eighty degrees to prepare a ten-minute speech!

I was, of course, used to the East African tradition of randomly inviting people to speak. But this seemed to take the practice to the extreme. I had no warning and nothing prepared—especially around people with a disability and HIV/AIDS. Stephen was very used to being my 'Aaron' to translate during my local preaching, but I still had to think up what to say.

What happened to me, as I frantically tried to pull together my thoughts, is not the point of the story. The point is that I was being included, and Stephen had become my enabler in my speech impairment, and my inability to speak Kimeru. The significance of this only dawned on me after returning to the UK when I reflected on the matter-of-fact way that Stephen responded to my impairments. It contrasted with the reactions I got back home.

In the UK there are developed services, anti-discrimination legislation and inclusive policies, but the vibes I often get are ones of embarrassment and having to make special arrangements. This is so different from the shrug-of-the-shoulders spontaneity in Kenya. But in Kenya it had not come immediately. Stephen, like all my friends and colleagues, had to get to know me. Then they could respond positively and include me in their groups. In many ways my very being in Kenya, and in this community, was teaching them how people with disability can contribute. We so often ask 'What can I bring to mission?' God is saying 'Just bring yourself and I'll do the rest.' In Kenya, I experienced a greater willingness than I have in the UK to move from a position of not knowing how to respond to a person with disabilities to one of inclusion and a 'can-do' approach to my impairments. In Kenya, once people knew me, I would find my *participation* was expected, whereas in the UK, it often seems that my presence is nothing more than accepted.

Stephen's 'can-do' approach was reflected in many of my Kenyan colleagues. They had learned, perhaps through having me around for long enough, that I was just one of them and could be included as any other in their cultural practices.

### *3. Bartimaeus and the Muthara Disabled People's Organization*

A third story comes from my visiting a group of people with disability to share a story from Mark's gospel, which came to life, in part, because of my disability. It is said that people's lived experience can provide a lens through which they read the Bible. Also that the reason for the gospel writer sharing the incident can be as important as the story itself. Both are true here.

One Saturday morning, I was invited to attend a meeting of people with disabilities in Muthara, a nearby market town. The group had recently become part of the Meru North DCC. As I sat at the front, I prayed about what I was going to say, and the name Bartimaeus kept coming into my head. I knew the story from Mark 10:46–52 well and realised that it could be quite fitting.

I spoke to the group about Bartimaeus, a blind man, begging by the roadside, feeling excluded from what was going on but deciding he wanted to meet Jesus. When he called out, the crowd rebuked him. He was an embarrassment and was not regarded as worthy of Jesus' attention. However, Bartimaeus persisted.

As I told this story, I could see that people were engaging with what I was saying. They knew how it felt to be sitting by the roadside, ignored. They knew what it was like to have to shout louder than everybody else to be heard. They knew what it was like to be discriminated against and to experience prejudice.

This story is often used as an example of Jesus' healing ministry. But it also describes people being excluded. These people have to shout out persistently to gain recognition. Finally, Jesus directly engages with this excluded man through the question 'What do you want me to do for you?' (Mark 10:51; Luke 18:41). The story is much more than just another miracle.

As the speaker, I identified with the hearers. We were discussing issues that were familiar to us all. I doubt that the same talk would have had the same effect had I not been a person with disability myself.

## The Outcomes of My Work in Kenya

Perhaps the biggest impact I made during my time in Kenya was simply in interacting with people—within the hospital, the town and wherever I happened to be. Regardless of what I *did*, the fact that I was there doing anything at all was a revelation to people, both Kenyans and expatriates. Being included is a small stepping stone for people with disability, but it can be frustrating and patronising when it stops there. The challenge is to move on from that place—easier to do in rural Africa than in the UK.

When disabled people show interest in serving in mission, the unspoken question on people's lips is 'But what can you offer?' Even now, thirteen years after I returned to the UK, that unspoken question remains. Yet just being there can be enough. We too often have a narrow perspective on what mission work entails, which can be disabling to people with disability.

There were times when I sat in my office and prayed 'Why am I here, God?' The answer came at the end of nine years of waiting, and on my return to Kenya, particularly to Maua. Action on Disability and Development chose not to start a separate programme in Kenya, but the Methodist programme that I started was taken over in 2002 by a Kenyan coordinator. Funding was provided through the British Methodist Church and then picked up by the World Council of Churches. The programme continued to work with people with disability, empowering them to live their own lives and to advocate for their needs. Its coordinator also got invited to speak to other Kenyan churches, thus cascading the impact of the small seed that I had played a part in sowing. Sadly, in 2017, I heard that the funding had come to an end. Its activities were being amalgamated into the Methodist Church's Development Department. However, the seed had, by that time, grown into a fully-fledged plant with structures and ideas that I hope the church will continue to nurture. I especially hope that the Disability Sunday will continue as part of the annual church calendar, to express God's mission to and through people with disabilities.

The Meru North Disability Community Centre (DCC) has been supported by various donors despite the ever-restricting funding environment. However, once again, God's mission through me was not so much to set up a Community-Based Rehabilitation (CBR) programme, but more to improve the infrastructure of services and self-help activities that will influence future development. I gave up my role as Director of the DCC when I returned to the UK in May 2005. I handed it over to the people with disability of Meru North, together with the Methodist Church in Kenya. I believe that this partnership has been fundamental to its survival.

God uses us in ways we often don't see at the time. Change can often be slow and painful, but progress is still being made. I believe my personal experience of disability has played a big part in the success of God's Mission in Meru North and the wider Methodist Church in Kenya.

## *Enabling Other Mission Partners with Disability*

I was always eager to meet others with disabilities who came to Kenya with short-term teams, but they were few and far between. I remember an American church of deaf people coming to Meru North on two or three occasions, and working with local schools and churches in our area. But I struggle to think of other examples.

We had been aware of Ros Colwill as a fellow Methodist mission partner working in Nigeria. She had trained social workers and assisted the development of a community project to support people experiencing mental illness. She had had a stroke whilst attending a family wedding in the UK. We had not been aware of her intention to return to Nigeria but were particularly pleased to hear that plans were in hand for this to happen.

As a wheelchair user, after her stroke, there had been some debate about whether Ros could return to Nigeria. However, the Methodist Church realised that they could also enable Ros by using the same system they had used for me in Kenya. Although Ros did not have the same communication impairments, many of her other support needs were similar. Ros returned to Nigeria as my family and I returned to the UK, and it made a huge impact on me, as it spoke so much of the inclusion I had been working to pioneer in Kenya.

## People with Disability and Christian Mission

The call to include people with disability in mission, and in the wider church, has gathered momentum over recent years. But are they 'accepted' or 'expected'? Do we simply accept them, saying, 'Well done for getting this far'? Or should we *expect* to see them, and ask where they are when they don't appear?

The 'care-only' mind-set has encouraged the 'common sense' view that can be disabling. Recalling Elinor Young's story, would it not have been deemed as 'common sense' that a teenager who walked with the help of shoulder crutches was not going to be much use in rural Indonesia? Is it not the same 'common sense' that makes us gloss over the fact that Moses had a speech impairment and needed a helper to enable him to carry out God's mission? It was certainly 'common sense' that, to start with, obstructed my progress towards working in rural Africa.

When people saw me operating as a mission partner, the 'care-only common sense' response often changed to saying 'yes, of course you can manage.' I think of a young woman with similar disabilities, who had never been outside the UK before Rachel and I invited her and her mother to help with a training project in Kenya. They now go out regularly, independently, to do further work. We need to rethink a theology of disability.

We pray the Lord's Prayer (Matthew 6:9–13), with its phrase, 'Your kingdom come' (verse 10). What does this mean for people with disability? On what terms are they part of the kingdom? People with disabilities have always been part of God's mission. This is not a twentieth and twenty-first century add-on. We now have airplanes, four-wheel-drive vehicles and computers, which were not previously available. These should enable people who may not have been previously considered.

People with disability may present themselves as teachers, doctors and ministers, and with other skills and attributes. We are called and gifted in the same way as the rest of Christ's church. We should not all become disability activists. The church needs to see people with disability as an asset rather than a burden, and embrace the unique skills and experiences they bring. To see God's kingdom coming will include people with disability as leaders and pioneers in the *missio Dei*!

CHAPTER 8

# People with Disabilities on Short-Term Mission

Jeff McNair
United States

## Introduction

What is the goal of a short-term mission trip? The Standards of Excellence in Short-Term Missions (STM) website states that there are seven standards of excellence in short term missions. These include being God centered, empowering partnerships and facilitating mutual design, comprehensive administration supervised by qualified leadership, appropriate training and thorough, thoughtful follow through and follow up.[1]

Thousands go on short-term mission trips each year. The work of these trips includes a wide range of activities. In my own church, people travel to provide day care for missionaries attending a renewal conference. They travel to Mexico to build small homes for families living in poverty. They have gone to other places to assist with upgrading an orphanage through cleaning, painting or simple construction. They may build ramps to make places accessible. Others teach a variety of topics, from English to the Bible, sharing their expertise. And others share professional expertise in education or medical care. These types of activities are all largely focused on providing a service to those on whom the mission is focused. Some types of services are obviously more specialized than others.

Whatever our capabilities, it is as Roger Peterson has observed:

> We have all been called to declare God's wonderful deeds—not just Jewish brethren, not just ecclesiastical professionals—but each one of us. Therefore, any Great Commission plan which falls short of potentially including the entire Body risks 'missing the mark' (*hamartia*, or sin) set by God.[2]

All can be involved in missions in some way. But in some circles, people with disabilities might not be given the chance. Disability often results in societal devaluation, simply because of an impairment, and how it is viewed. The experience of persons with disabilities cannot be explained exclusively on the basis of their bodily/functional impairments.[3] As the social model of disability explains, environments react to differences in socially constructed ways.[4] These reactions have been referred to as the social consequences of disability or as 'societal wounding.'[5] This form of discrimination finds its way into every facet of social interaction, including the church. Exclusion can be witnessed in many programs and activities of the church. To see it in our understanding and practice in missions should not surprise us. It is too easily assumed that persons with disabilities are not fit for mission service.

Consider the typical short-term missions team. How often are people with physical disabilities, intellectual disabilities, or other forms of impairment given the chance to participate? Do we send out teams which are heterogeneous in terms of race, gender and social status, while including persons with disabilities? Might we be missing out on potential outcomes? What benefits might we be losing? To include those with intellectual disabilities, or wheelchair users, would communicate a powerful message to the team and those they are serving.

## Who Should Go on Short-Term Mission Trips?

This question of inclusion is less about the characteristics of a person and more about what the rest of the team is willing to do to facilitate their participation. To embrace a disabled team member speaks volumes about those on the team. We have seen families on short-term mission trips go to extra effort to include their children who might need extra help. Are we willing to extend the same increased support to persons with disabilities? I have seen some people on short-term teams who were incontinent and needed assistance with toileting and other hygienic needs. They needed assistance to get into vehicles or to move around the worksite. Others with intellectual disabilities needed increased supervision and direction. One man who had a history of chronic absence seizures needed to be monitored in case he fell. Another team member was assigned to partner with him to prevent harm in the case of a seizure.

In each case, having team members with these characteristics made those who were being served step up, seeing how they could serve the mission team while being served by them. Thus, a variety of people were engaged in assisting someone to achieve their often life-changing goal of being able to serve others in a real way. It is as described in 1 Corinthians

12:22–23: 'On the contrary, those parts of the body that seem to be weaker are indispensable, and the parts that we think are less honorable we treat with special honour.' We include those who seem to be weaker, and so benefit from their indispensability. We include those parts of the body we think less honourable (God forgive us) and show them special honour by enabling them to express their gifts.

Including people in this way encourages reflection in those looking on. Exclusion communicates volumes. The person being served sees the typical, homogenously unimpaired group arriving to provide service and, perhaps unconsciously, has their discriminatory attitudes affirmed. But when we include people with disability, we are communicating, 'We brought someone with us who has a disability because we see them as a person of value. Disability does not disqualify someone from being gifted or expressing their gifting.' It also creates an opportunity to ask the locals, 'Where are the people with these types of characteristics in your community? Do you see them as people of value as well? Might we meet them?' The simple presence of team members with disabilities silently confronts societal norms. We may not even need to say anything, although we probably should raise the questions.

The presence of team members with disabilities can also challenge the 'moral model of disability' which is held by many in the places where short-termers go.[6] That is, disability is punishment for sin on someone's part. This is a serious myth that needs to be dispelled. To have people with disability on the team will demonstrate they are not a cause for shame, but rather equals—God's image bearers, team members and people included in work in a faraway place because of their value and what they have to offer.

The locals with disabilities, who have often been devalued, may have cause to reflect. 'Perhaps I could do more. Perhaps I could be put to work. I want to go and meet this team. These foreigners are not ashamed of team members who are disabled like me.' They will notice the different mind-set or worldview they are observing.

In an article entitled "Disability Studies Applied to Disability Ministry," I addressed a social model understanding of disability.[7] Discrimination can be viewed as the social consequence of disability. Team members with disabilities confront basic understandings of what disability is. Yes, disability is a characteristic of an individual, but responding to it becomes a characteristic of those around them. The personal reflection of mission team members and of those being served addresses inherent—often unconscious—discrimination. When a person with disability takes part, it changes the perceptions of other team members, and their own self-perception about what they can accomplish. When these people can express their gifting, we may gain a better understanding of God's purpose for them individually, and for the larger body of Christ.

In addition, people with family members who have a disability will ask, 'Who is this God that sees people with disabilities as having value? Maybe I will bring out my son/brother/daughter/aunt to meet the team.' In several places, people affected by disability will say they read *Joni*, Joni Eareckson Tada's autobiography. Learning of her faith in the face of quadriplegia, they are moved to say, 'I want to follow the God of Joni!'

Those with disability themselves are often the most effective at reaching out to others with disability. They bring a natural empathy, a point of connection, despite being from a different culture, socioeconomic status, and having a different education level. It is like two people who speak the same language meeting in a foreign place.

At the Joni and Friends organization, people with physical disabilities routinely go on mission trips. Videos of these trips vividly display their impact on the rest of the team, and on those they meet with disabilities. Designing trips to include team members with disabilities requires a unique approach logistically. Just like the other team members, their strengths and abilities need to be discovered and brought out. People with disabilities may not at first see their gifting, depending on the opportunities provided for them in their church or working life. If a role on a team is something new, training in areas that might be obvious to others needs to be reinforced. On one mission trip, a team member with intellectual disabilities boarded the wrong bus and was 'lost' for over an hour. He did not realize the importance of staying with his team. Others were frantic in trying to find him. He had simply followed friendly members of another team who were going to a different location. Knowing how such misunderstandings occur can be made clear before the trip. Extra thought needs to be given to foresee difficulties, and to support those with disabilities.

People on the team, and in the location being served, will need to assist. Those supporting the people with disability may be unsure of what to do, and will need to be shown. This will benefit them in the longer term for their own social context.

## A Case Study

Let me describe a mission trip that was planned to include persons affected by disabilities. The idea began when I spoke at a church where staff of a ministry called 'Hands of Mercy' worshipped. Hands of Mercy builds houses for poor families in Mexico. Parts of the houses are fabricated at a US location like a church, and then assembled in Mexico on-site in one day. The sermon was delivered on what was called 'Disability Sunday,' which happened every few years. Based upon 1 Corinthians 12, I emphasized the need for the body of Christ to be connected in all activities. There was a large adult Sunday class which included members with various disabilities. The Hands of Mercy staff wondered about the possibility of class members participating on a trip to build a house. This would include putting together separate parts of the house at the church and then assembling them in Mexico.

First we explained to them the time, money and stamina that would be needed. The group had several with intellectual disabilities, one with severe physical disability and a man with multiple disabilities. Five volunteered and became part of a team of twenty-four who prepared and assembled a house for a poor woman living outside of Ensenada, Mexico.

The team was helped to prepare for including these participants, but they were not entirely aware of what the trip would entail. Typically, the aim of these trips is to provide a home for someone 'devalued' by poverty. The recipient is blessed by the home, and the team by their service in providing it. But this time was different, for the team had also provided a unique opportunity for socially devalued people to take on a valued role (missionary, philanthropist, assistant to the poor, etc.). They were doubly blessed.

Team members with disabilities needed to be assisted in and out of vans, and other team members had to be their buddies. All parties rose to the occasion, entering into this arrangement with their eyes open. Through the participation of members with disabilities, everyone came to see people with disabilities in an entirely different manner.

First the church had to overcome intellectual barriers such as wondering whether it even made sense to include persons with disabilities in such a venture. The team had to show patience to those who moved slowly, and those who didn't understand, or could not do the same kind or amount of work as they. Some people needed help with personal hygiene/toileting.

It was particularly lovely to see the woman who was receiving the home assisting team members with disabilities. Not only did team members help each other, but they received ministry themselves. It is a beautiful thing to go to someone you are serving, and in humility provide the chance for that person to take pride in also serving you.

Tasks that were doable by persons with an impairment were reserved for them, but the work they did was real work. One task that needed to be done was to help the woman receiving the house to select curtains. Our team member who had physical disability also had an eye for decorating, and met with her to discuss decorating plans. This resulted in a lovely interaction as they discussed how interior decoration, from floor tile to paint to draperies, would help to make the house a home. It was one of the few times our team members interacted closely with people in the community. Through this, the locals saw people with disability contribute, and overcome. They saw a man with a seizure disorder not allowing it to keep him from serving. They saw a beautiful, indomitable friendliness and skill brought to a board game by a woman with an intellectual disability. They saw loving marital relationships between adults with intellectual disabilities. They saw how people with intellectual disabilities could have a deep understanding of spiritual matters. They saw a willingness in team members to serve others as best as they could, in spite of their limitations. As one of the team members said, 'I can't do everything, but I can do something.'

Of course there were challenges; these were mainly seen in those without disabilities. It wasn't easy for members to take on responsibilities perhaps atypical for a short-term mission trip. Although we did our best to prepare for any eventualities, some things happened that were unforeseen. When someone who has limited physical movement develops travel diarrhea, others on the team need to step up and assist. Handling a wheelchair on a rural building site can be difficult. People with intellectual disabilities may not understand what is required of them on the first, second or third time it is explained. As with any group, there may be personality clashes. People who have not had experiences with disabilities may be thrown by mental illness, or behavioural issues, or non-compliance with social conventions. These are challenges, but they are also opportunities to grow.

We are not surprised when parents take their children on a short-term trip, but still expect the child to pitch in as they are able. People with disabilities are not children, but their involvement, as they are able, can show what they can achieve. Including people with disability is about an investment. Some elements of that investment would not otherwise occur. Too many churches, let alone mission projects, are unwilling to make this investment, or perhaps it just doesn't occur to them to do it, so they do not experience the unique benefits they would reap; benefits they have not even imagined.

## Closing Reflections

With a change in mind-set about who might join a short-term mission trip, people can have new expectations. We begin with the same goals that any mission trip begins with, and most importantly to share the gospel of Christ, but the mission itself quickly expands:

- To teach team members about the lives of people living with disabilities.
- To provide persons with disabilities with real ministry opportunities.
- To assemble the whole body of Christ for ministry.
- To provide opportunities for service to those who are being served.
- To value devalued people and treat all people with respect.
- To be hospitable.
- To change the lives of all team members, not just as it relates to mission activities but regarding people with disabilities in any context.
- To impact the perception of persons with disabilities bringing cultural change where mission activities are being hosted.

We don't advocate change simply for change's sake. But if we have been in error or have limited the works of God through our traditions, we must reflect on ways in which things might be different.

CHAPTER 9

# Weak to Weaker: For Children with Disabilities across the Globe

Natalie Flickner
Crisis Care Training International
United States

'No way!' I said out loud while opening my second email from Phyllis Kilbourn. Winter, my dog, lifted her head at the sound of my voice in our quiet home in South Carolina. I had already said no to Phyllis's first email regarding writing a curriculum.

*Who even wants to write a curriculum? I don't. This opportunity is still a sure no!* I thought as I quickly closed her email.

Frustrated, I sat back on our couch, and my eyes met those of sweet Winter. *Lord, please use me for your kingdom*, I prayed, like I had so many times and years before.

*No way*. There it came again. Not from doubt this time, but rather from an immediate realization that God was answering my lifelong prayers in that moment. He was answering me with this invitation.

## Birth

On a cold December evening in 1980, my mom and dad stepped into the local hospital to give birth to their second baby. Quickly, after thirty minutes of delivery, my mother held me in her arms. The birth process had gone well and I appeared like an ideal newborn, so much so that the delivery doctor gave me an eleven on the Apgar scale, a perfect score.

The time came for the nurse to clean me up, so my mom confidently placed me in the nurse's arms. My parents expected the nurse to bring me back to them in a few minutes. However, after considerable time, the doctor appeared empty-handed. Something had gone terribly wrong. He told my parents that I had been left in my hospital crib unattended and when I was found I was not breathing. The doctor had resuscitated me by mouth-to-mouth as a nurse watched on with paralyzing fear.

Within those critical moments, my brain was starved of oxygen, resulting in mild brain damage in the motor control area of the brain—mild cerebral palsy. The doctor explained to my parents that their new baby girl would have a gaited walk, and difficulties with speech and with fine motor skills throughout life.

Over my lifetime, I've deeply thought about those critical moments without oxygen that quickly passed away, but shaped my life and my family forever. However, as I now begin looking at the life that could have been, my heart shifts to the truth that I know: God, my God, was there with me and holding me within those life-defining moments. He was not absent, but rather he was sovereignly in control and loving me fully in those moments.

As an adult, I can now look back and realize that God was beginning a bigger story in my life that would involve world missions and reaching other children with disabilities around the world for his name.

But long before I could understand the bigger story that God had planned for me, I had to learn to acquire basic skills and live in a world that often shuns differences.

## Childhood

I first met Carol, a speech pathologist, at the age of two. My parents took me to see her due to my lack of speech. Carol's goal was to develop my language skills and work on correct pronunciation. I remember her office floor covered with Fisher-Price toys. The toys were there to engage my attention and to draw out my speech. 'We bought every toy we could just to try to get you to talk,' my mom has said multiple times.

Since the tongue is a muscle, it was affected by my cerebral palsy. I've often warned people that my tongue has a mind of its own, even after enduring years of training. Carol would place peanut butter around my lips and face to entice my tongue to move in a correct way. School was a battle on many fronts, fought by my parents, Carol and me. I was the first child with multiple physical needs to be mainstreamed in the school district. After many meetings and disagreements, my mom and Carol helped to prove that my needs were related to my educational wellbeing. In response, the school provided additional speech therapy, occupational therapy and physical therapy for me.

My biggest difficulty in school was handwriting. Due to my motor skills, writing was terribly slow and laborious. During third grade, I started typing on a typewriter provided by the school. That black typewriter followed me until twelfth grade.

Along with the tedious therapies during and after school and overwhelming homework, being physically different from other children created a painful thorn in my heart. I'll never forget the day when I was first called a retard. I was in first grade, standing in line behind two girls from another class.

'Are you a retard?' Alison asked as two girls stared at me intensely.

Feeling their hostility toward me, I honestly said 'Um . . . I don't know. What is a retard?' They placed their hands to their chests and purposely hit their chests, like so many other kids in the school would do as I walked by. I told my classroom teacher, not because I was a tell-tale, but because I wanted to understand what a 'retard' was, since it was obviously related to me. This led to my having to identify the girls to teachers. A note was sent home to my parents, and I saw the hurt in my mom's eyes as she explained the meaning of 'retard' to me.

In fifth grade, our family changed churches. I knew of Jesus' death and resurrection, but I had never known him as my personal Saviour. He changed my world. The bitterness of being teased and excluded suddenly disappeared and was replaced by a Friend who would never leave me. He became my life.

## Calling to Missions

During sixth grade I was a part of the Awana Clubs at church. Awana is a Bible club for children that focuses on memorizing verses of Scripture. Along with memorizing, we were encouraged to explore activities that focused on serving and helping. One project was interviewing a missionary in our church. I interviewed Suzie, a missionary recently returned from the field. Suzie, who had a close relative with cerebral palsy, wanted to spend time with me. For the next two years, with my parents' permission, Suzie took me out to eat (always pizza) once a week. During these outings, Suzie and I would talk about people's need for the gospel and how I could share my faith at school. From sixth grade on, I knew without a shadow of a doubt that God wanted me to go to Bible college and become a missionary.

During this time, I was blessed to be part of a very active church and youth group that exposed us to world missions. The missions conference quickly became one of my most anticipated events in the year. I even went so far as to ask my school teachers for homework ahead of time, so I would be able to attend most of the conference. The summer before ninth grade, I distinctly remember chasing down my youth group pastor and saying, 'When can I apply for the high school Mexico trip?' My youth pastor paused and smiled, saying, 'Natalie, you have to wait one more year.'

While waiting for Mexico, I went to South Dakota with my youth group that summer to help with Bible School for children living on the Indian Reservation. We also went to paint houses. Once there, ready to help paint a house, the youth leaders and I suddenly realized that painting required the ability to be steady on a ladder. Walking toe-to-toe in a straight line on the floor was a challenge for me, so the ladder was clearly off limits! The house did have another obvious need: the yard had garbage everywhere. For the next two or three days, from 8:30 to 4:30, while everyone else painted, I picked up every bit of trash in that yard. To be honest, my heart struggled. I wanted to do what everyone else did, alongside of others. I wanted to take part in the big and the important, but God wanted me to serve him within my physical limits, not outside or in spite of them.

Finally, I went to Mexico with my youth group, and I was thrilled to go to another culture and share the gospel. Our team of eight high schoolers and two adults spent weeks before the trip practising mimes and puppet shows that we later presented at a local Mexican church during their summer vacation bible school.

Our team was hosted by a missionary couple: Katie and Stan. To my surprise, Stan had mild cerebral palsy. One afternoon, Stan invited me on a short walk to find an ice-cold Coke. He then shared with me that after seminary training he had applied to over one hundred churches to be a pastor. He explained that some churches never replied to his application, while one church bluntly said, 'We need our pastor to throw a football.' God then led them to missions and opened the doors for them. Stan said 'Natalie, if God is calling you to be a missionary, he will make a way for you.' I have never forgotten Stan's words to me, nor the testimony of his life.

During high school, the story of Gideon became my heart's hidden hope. In Judges 6, when God called Gideon to serve him, Gideon describes himself, 'My clan is the weakest in Manasseh, and I am the least in my family' (v. 15). No one would ever expect that the God of Israel would choose to use the weakest of the weak to save Israel from their oppressors. Gideon's story was my assurance that God is a God who sees the inner heart, and that God chooses what the world quickly disregards. Gideon's and my God is the God of the impossible.

## Training for Missions

After completing high school, God clearly directed me through my desire to study the Bible and pursue full-time foreign missions. So my parents, who completely supported me, drove me twelve hours away from our home to attend Columbia International University. For the first time in my life, I felt like I fit in, that I belonged. The infectious warmth and acceptance of the professors, staff and students was unlike anything I had experienced before. I majored in both Bible and intercultural studies (missions). Homework was indeed a challenge but nevertheless a joy and delight.

During my first year at CIU, the year's verse was Ephesians 3:20, 'Now to him who is able to do far more abundantly than all that we ask or think, according to the power at work within us' (ESV). When I entered chapel almost daily, I saw this verse hung high and started to realize that I was seeing my God do more for me than I had ever imagined.

I met a young man, Kevin Flickner, the very first day of freshmen orientation. Kevin grew up as a missionary kid mostly in South Korea and South Africa. Kevin and I ended up having all but one class together, our halls were paired together for social activities and we were even in the same small group as freshmen. We quickly became friends, especially since so much of our daily routine was identical.

The name 'Kevin' means 'kind, gentle and loveable.' I have never in the past or present met a person so kind, gentle and, without a doubt, so lovable. His quick wit and unique humour kept me laughing and wanting more time with him. He was willing to get to know me for who God made me. At times it was uncanny how Kevin instinctively knew how to help me with my physical needs like carrying a tray, cutting my food or walking slower for me. My family and friends were amazed at Kevin's sensitive attention towards me that never seemed to wane.

Kevin and I married less than a month after our college graduation. Our wedding was a celebration testifying to the goodness and greatness of God. God opened the door at CIU for Kevin to attend seminary, as he did for many other Bible college graduates preparing to serve overseas. Kevin's parents were still ministering in South Africa at a Bible college, training local students. During college Kevin and I had completed a summer internship together under his parents. The time in South Africa led us to have a similar vision of ministry for our future. We were on mission and by God's grace I was a missionary, albeit short-term.

## Further Weakening like Gideon

While watching God accomplish so much in my life—college graduation, marriage, short-term mission and expected long-term overseas mission work—I assumed that God had won the battle in my life just as he had in Gideon's story. However, God does not promise us the immediate, glowing victory that we often deeply desire. Instead, God often allows further weakness in our lives so that he receives unquestionable glory, just as he did for Gideon in Judges 7 by taking a twenty-two-thousand-man army and whittling it down to only three hundred men. God wanted the victory ahead to be without a doubt a glowing testament to his divine hand, his presence and his deliverance of his people.

God began the painful process of further weakening me during our second year of marriage. It began with fatigue, joint pain and depression. I was working part-time at a local church preschool while Kevin worked three part-time jobs as well as attending seminary. In childhood, I had always tired easily. I needed naps after school or breaks during physical exertion like hiking or canoeing with family and friends. However, this new fatigue in my twenties was a different type of beast, unlike anything that I had felt before.

As a child I overcame through skill building, repetition, sheer determination and proper rest. To my complete dismay, none of these methods could cut or lessen the fatigue that I was experiencing. The simple task of taking a shower left me feeling exhausted, and at times I would need to lie down after showering. I went from living a productive life as a wife and part-time worker with multiple daily responsibilities to having the daily goals of showering and washing dishes.

The depression was not something new in my life. I had experienced it before as a teenager. Being so vulnerable emotionally and mentally while living with mild cerebral palsy was difficult, and nothing I wanted to repeat. However, as God had done before and continues to do, he held my hand and carried me through.

The moment I could no longer work, God provided a full-time job for Kevin at the CIU library, allowing him to finish seminary part-time. God's provision for us at that time spoke volumes to us. We were surprised by my new physical situation, and did not know what its full effects would be, but through God's amazing provision, we knew that God was going ahead of us, forging the way for us.

The onslaught of doctors and tests began. All the tests only revealed how healthy I was. The disparity between the doctors' reports and my low ability to function was shocking and devastating to me. I began to question the reality of my symptoms, whether they were real or in my head. With Kevin's support and the Lord's strength, I slowly began to trust what my body was saying to me and began the lengthy process of learning to live within the limits of these new symptoms.

The way I envisioned our lives, especially future mission work, drastically changed. It felt as though what God had called me to as a young teenager was falling further and further away. Preparing to minister in Jesus' name in another country while living with mild cerebral palsy would be challenging and risky in many ways, but living overseas with fatigue and joint pain alongside the challenges of cerebral palsy seemed completely impossible for now.

One morning, I woke up with my eye looking as red as an apple. A quick run to the doctor, a quick diagnosis, no big deal, right? The only problem was that my eye never completely cleared of the redness. Seeing one eye doctor led to being referred to another. Finally, I received a correct diagnosis of iritis and uveitis, often called arthritis of the eye. It is simply inflammation in the eye causing redness, pain and sensitivity to light.

Before these new eye issues began, I had started taking seminary classes in spiritual formation and pastoral counselling. Due to my eye problems, my vision was blurry, causing me to shuffle between two pairs of glasses while reading and typing papers for finals. While doing this shuffle dance, I erupted into laughter. I had no clue what was happening to me physically—before diagnosis—or why God was allowing more and more suffering in my life. At the same time, during so many unknowns and struggles, I knew that he was near to me, holding me close to himself.

After living with unexplained fatigue and joint pain for over four years, those symptoms were finally linked to my eye problems, and together linked to a specific gene causing systemic inflammation in my body. To my relief, I began medication. For the first time in years, my every activity and decision was not dictated by my level of fatigue.

Around this time, I learned that the eye inflammation damaged an area of my right eye, resulting in glaucoma. The glaucoma specialist sat back in his chair and said to me, 'I have to be blunt with you.' This is never a statement anyone wants to hear from a doctor. He continued, 'Most people get glaucoma later in life, in their seventies and eighties. People usually don't have glaucoma in their early thirties. It will be difficult for us to keep your eyesight throughout your life. You will have multiple eye surgeries in life, glaucoma will spread to your other eye, and blindness is inevitable.' I was completely shocked. My first eye surgery followed shortly.

God whittled Gideon's army to three hundred. I felt whittled down to near nothing.

## God's Assignment

Even after being whittled, there was one significant difference between Gideon's story and mine. God had assigned Gideon's battlefield. My heart longed to serve God, to have a specific assignment from God. Just as I did in high school, I chose to cling to the truth that God sees the inner heart and that he delights in using the weakest to bring glory to himself. I didn't know my exact assignment in God's kingdom; but I prayed, hoped and still waited for that specific assignment.

After completing my master's in pastoral counselling, I began to sense through prayer that God was pointing me to use my counselling training by writing. I shared with a friend from our church my desire to write in some capacity. Beyond my expectations, weeks later my friend called saying that she had learned of a ministry called Crisis Care Training International that needed writers.

When Phyllis Kilbourn, the founder of CCTI, first emailed me asking me to write a module about children with disabilities, I had no interest in writing such a curriculum. Three months later, Phyllis emailed me again, asking me to reconsider. I was very surprised to hear from Phyllis again and realized that God wanted me to take a closer look at this ministry opportunity.

The day Kevin and I met Phyllis Kilbourn and Rosemary Sabatino, the director of CCTI, was like the turning over of a tapestry to reveal a precious pattern that God was weaving into my life from the start. For most of my life, I had always seen the back of the tapestry with loose strings that never matched and awkward-sized knots. The loose strings and awkward knots were cerebral palsy, numerous other struggles in childhood, a questionable call to missions, depression and chronic illness. But as I sat listening to the ministry of CCTI and began to understand the purpose of their curriculum, God flipped over the tapestry to reveal his intricate design that I had never seen before: he had been preparing me for ministry to children with disabilities throughout the world.

Crisis Care Training International is a ministry under World Evangelization for Christ (WEC). CCTI's mission is to bring the hope of Jesus to children in crisis through training and resources. When Phyllis Kilbourn was a missionary in Liberia, she saw firsthand the traumatic effects a war could have on children. It was this experience that God used to lead Phyllis to see and to understand the need to train caregivers about children in crisis. Several groups of children are known as children in crisis: children of war, street children, sexually exploited children, children in orphanages and children with disabilities. CCTI has a curriculum comprised of different modules. Most of the modules focus on a specific group of children in crisis and their unique needs. CCTI also develops curriculum teachers who meet set standards, both in material knowledge and Christian character.

At that time, when we first met, Phyllis Kilbourn had recently edited and published a book called *Let All the Children Come: A Handbook for Holistic Ministry to Children with Disabilities.* CCTI needed a writer to write the module on children with disabilities, and they were looking specifically for a writer with personal experience in disability. The writing project would need to follow the curriculum pattern as a fifteen-lesson module focused on the needs of children with disabilities. Then, after writing the curriculum, CCTI would use both Phyllis's book and the fifteen-lesson module to train caregivers throughout the world. CCTI offers training to caregivers, through their trained teachers, in three ways: on-site across the world, through university classes and online. Phyllis usually allows a writer one year but was willing to give me two.

Just as God used Gideon to rid his fellow Israelite countrymen of the oppression of Midian, God's mission for me was to participate in exposing the often unseen and unacknowledged oppression of children with disabilities. I know the inner heart of a child with a disability not because I completed another degree, but because I was one myself. As I agreed to the commitment of writing the module I was overwhelmed by God's love and wisdom in offering me an opportunity to serve him in missions that is interwoven with my own life and suffering. God used the additional weakening in my life to prepare me to better understand, and identify with, the extensive global oppression of children with disabilities.

## Children with Disabilities

Before CCTI, I had seldom heard the terms 'crisis' and 'trauma' used in relation to children with disabilities. However, understanding trauma and crisis from a pastoral angle and reflecting on my own childhood experiences helped me understand how a childhood disability is in fact a crisis for a child. A childhood disability is a crisis because of one word: loss. A disability in childhood affects every part of a child's life: emotionally, socially, educationally, physically and spiritually—and it even affects their families. A child with a disability withstands more losses than one without disability, resulting in grief and placing them at an additional risk for more emotional consequences.

Children with disabilities are in every town, every country, every continent; but their daily plight is continually ignored by cultures, leaders and even Jesus' own followers. We know through the gospel writers that Jesus chose to touch the leper, bend down to the lame, wash the eyes of the blind and notice the unnoticeable. Yet even after two thousand years of the church reading and studying Jesus' life, people with disability remain one of the largest unreached groups in the world. The Lausanne Movement estimates that only 5–10 percent of those with disability have been effectively reached with the gospel. The stark reality of these two truths—Jesus' life and the present exclusion of people with disabilities from the gospel—is a dichotomy that too few care to notice.[1]

Around the world children with disabilities are also inclined to live in poverty, to have poor access to physical therapy and health services, and to rarely receive a full education.[2] An inadequate education equals loss of skills, jobs and the means of livelihood, or any personal independence as an adult, often leaving them in poverty. A cycle of poverty results. Around the globe, children with disabilities spend their lives lying on dirt floors, painfully scooting their bodies on the floor just to move, and enduring lives without developing speech skills.

Children with disabilities also experience lives of prejudice, discrimination, social exclusion and often abuse. Kids were cruel to me. But I had my parents and others as strong advocates standing beside me. In many cultures, however, instead of these children being supported, they are rejected and even abused. They live in isolation, shame and fear of further rejection.

Currently in some cultures, many churches do not even welcome children with disabilities in their fellowship because of false beliefs that these children are demon-possessed. In contrast, the mission movement can reach out to this most marginalized group. Christian caregiving, whether by a parent, a church helper, a worker at an orphanage or a teacher at a residential day-school, can intervene in the life of a child with a disability through compassion, kindness, acceptance, care and an authentic trusting relationship. We can foster an environment to further build inclusion for the child in their school, church and in the community.

Children with disabilities need to be loved and accepted by the body of Christ, so that they can hear and experience the powerful and saving name of Jesus. I have come to realize that my own experience in growing up with a disability paves a path to relate powerfully to children and adults with disabilities. Through this, by God's sovereignty, he has given me this cultural understanding, in order that I might play a role in reaching this unreached people group. Through my cultural understanding of disability, my mission to equip missionaries to reach out to those with disability is being played out.

## Valuable Lessons about Disability and Mission

Writing this module, and pursuing the mission God had given me, has taught me a lot about disability and mission. And perhaps these lessons are relevant for others with disability, and agencies working with people with disability on mission. Actually, perhaps some of my learnings are relevant for all missionaries as they seek to serve God, despite or even through their weaknesses, as they depend on God's power in weakness!

When I began writing the module, I thought that I could perhaps write a lesson in a week. Now, I laugh at that thought, as it took me between three-and-a-half and four years to finish writing. At times, my progress in writing was painfully slow. I continued to struggle with fatigue, tiredness and side effects from the arthritis medication. It often seemed that when I was gaining momentum in writing, sickness or fatigue would derail my ability to focus and write. Again, Phyllis and Rosemary graciously and patiently allowed me the extra time to complete the module. The lesson learned here, when considering serving in mission, is that people with disability will often need more time. And to facilitate their mission, the patience of those around them, such as family and mission agencies, is important. Phyllis and Rosemary never once pressured me for a deadline, but rather they have been God's voice of rest and unending grace. Months after I had started the work, Rosemary asked me to join the CCTI team. To say that I was excited is a complete understatement! As I completed the application process to become an associate member of WEC, I was in awe of God's calling and faithfulness to me in making me a missionary. The Lord has answered my childhood prayers.

I wish I could say that writing is a natural talent. However, due to the way God created me, and perhaps to my struggle with speech and language, putting my thoughts and feelings into words is not always easy for me. Once I began the project, I knew that I was unable to write even one sentence in my own strength. This knowledge, and the reality of my struggle with writing, drove me deeper in my relationship with God. Through this project I have begun to learn the art of waiting on God while resting in God. Time and time again God would ask me to lay aside the task of writing to just rest in him in silence or with music. The verse Isaiah 30:15b says 'in repentance and rest is your salvation, in quietness and trust is your strength.' This verse repeatedly guided me to lay down my desire to be productive, and to enjoy his peaceful presence. God faithfully reminded me as I wrote, regardless of the amount I wrote, that he was always with me and would never leave me. At times in my mind's eye, I would picture Jesus standing behind me as I wrote, with his powerful hands on my shoulders and his chin resting on the top of my head. To me each word, each sentence, each paragraph and each lesson became not just something to do *for* God, but something to do *with* God. Disability in mission has an important role in growing a deep dependence on God, where his power shines through our weakness.

After writing five out of fifteen lessons (one year of writing) I distinctively remember looking at the phone and wanting to call Phyllis or Rosemary and say, 'I quit.' It was too difficult and took too long. At that moment God reminded me of the stories of children with disabilities all over the world that I had read during my research. Then, I remembered the painful challenges of growing up with cerebral palsy. My journey gave me a deep empathy for children across the world. Only almighty God could have uniquely skilled me through my own experience of disability and then given me this opportunity and this assignment. Indeed, God has a perfect way of equipping us and preparing us for service, through our struggles and weaknesses. Saying 'I quit' was not an option for me. My only option was to live and write by God's never-ending grace.

Team meetings, retreats and annual conferences have opened times for priceless friendships to grow and flourish. The CCTI team and greater WEC community has indeed become additional family to me. This module to help caregivers understand the needs of children with disabilities started with Phyllis's vision to find someone with personal experience with a disability to write this module. Without CCTI's and WEC's willingness to accept and enfold me in their family, this module could never have been completed as envisioned. These bodies are a model for mission agencies to imitate in making an environment for people with disability to serve and flourish. Their gentle guidance has allowed me to explore how God would use my disability. Further, CCTI's support, along with the support of my loving husband, friends and supporters, has reinforced to me what all missionaries need to remember: interdependence. We can't serve alone in ministry, and especially not in missions. Disability reinforces (or even forces) a healthy awareness of our interdependency.

While writing the module and serving on CCTI's team, I had other opportunities to serve as well. God gave me the strength, boldness and grace to speak on a panel two years in a row at a conference attended mostly by doctors and medical professionals serving in world missions. In God's sovereignty, these speaking opportunities further blossomed into additional writing assignments regarding children with disabilities. CCTI also trained me to teach the curriculum. In fact, I have taught the first module, 'Children in Crisis,' twice as an eight-week online course. God is leading CCTI to prepare me to teach the module 'Restoring Hope for Children with Disabilities' to caregivers and missionaries as we watch God multiply the training, as other trained teachers share the module around the world. I guess disability has protected me from the conceit of thinking that I could do it all, and instead made me focus on the training of others, which has in turn multiplied the mission.

In one sense God's mission for me, that is, writing the module, is complete, but in another way the assignment has just begun. It is time to take the module to other people and to other nations. I have poured so much of myself into this project, but it is time to watch and learn from caregivers themselves as they interact with the material. In the future, I would love to teach this module overseas in whatever capacity God has planned for me. At the same time, I have learned to live holding future dreams very lightly, while also expecting God to do the impossible. Regardless of the future, God has graciously allowed me to realize the calling to missions he placed on my heart as a young girl.

While our CCTI ministry through this module is to teach and train others in how to engage effectively with children with disabilities, we must respect other cultures, be willing to learn from others and be ready to adapt ourselves—and the module—to their needs. I have experienced a childhood disability, lived years as an adult with additional physical trials, and spent years researching and writing, but I am not an expert in this area. I am still a learner. I will need to yield myself continually to the Lord so that others can better hear what God needs to teach them about children with disabilities, while at the same time growing as a strong and powerful advocate for children with disabilities. I don't know exactly what my ongoing role in mission will be. But as I look back on God's faithfulness, I can look forward with anticipation to how he will use my disability for his mission.

CHAPTER 10

# Deciding to Go on Mission with Disability

Justin Reimer
The Elisha Foundation and
Grace Bible Church of Bend
Ukraine

## Our Story

Disability became resident in our lives with the birth of our first child, Elisha (Eli), in June of 1997. The Lord shaped us by Eli's life from the very moment we learned he had Down syndrome. His birth opened a whole new world to us. We were planning to head into full-time, cross-cultural ministry leading up to his birth. With his birth we quickly realized that our mission field had changed and that raising a child with special needs was our new stewardship and calling. Little did we know that one day this calling would overlap with our former plan, and meld into one of the more challenging decisions we've made.

In 2005 we set up The Elisha Foundation, encouraging families experiencing disability. We worked primarily in North America, but also came alongside missionaries and churches cross-culturally. Through this the Lord began to stir our hearts once more towards a greater commitment in overseas ministry. Through Bible-saturated prayer, the pursuit of wise counsel, and a new evaluation of our circumstances, it became clear that we were to move our family to Ukraine to help advance ministry to people with disabilities.

Moving one's family overseas is a difficult process for any family: preparing to engage a new culture, weighing educational options, planning logistics, and preparing to leave behind all that is familiar. Having a child with special needs increases the difficulty significantly. Explaining to our families and friends that we would be transitioning to ministry overseas was met with obvious concern. Why move your family to a place vastly under-resourced? What about Eli's friends and relationships in the States?

These questions were prompted by care for our family and a particular love for Eli. We were grateful for this care. The response from friends and family was helpful in creating a sort of grid to evaluate various aspects of the decision process. Since our family dynamic was unique, we needed to confront conventional wisdom with a well-reasoned and godly response. But conventional wisdom is not necessarily godly wisdom! Conventional wisdom said we shouldn't have other children after Eli. Conventional wisdom argues that one should place their child with special needs only in the best possible location for receiving every imaginable resource. But that argument elevates resources above the value of that child's God-given abilities.

Our prayer and wisdom-seeking revolved around the following:

1. The word of God gives all we need for life and godliness (1 Timothy 3:16). We sought to establish a biblical confidence in our decision-making.
2. Eli is a person, a distinct image-bearer of God, and we must thoughtfully consider all that makes up *who* he is rather than simply defining him by *what* he has (i.e., Down syndrome).
3. Sacrifice is often associated with the Christian definition of 'missionary.'
4. We needed to consider practical matters and how to build supports specific to his needs.

## What We Believe and Have Learned

### *Living in the Image of God (*Imago Dei*)*

We are created in the image of God (Genesis 1:26–27) and therefore every human being is an image-bearer of God. We call this *imago Dei* (image of God). God has perfectly and clearly established all humans as above all earthly things (Genesis 1:28–31; Psalm 8:3–8). Humans are above all things without exception, so even those with disabilities are created with the same position, which reflects God's glory, though this world is stained by the Fall (Romans 8:18–25). Sin has marred our world but has not detracted from the worth or value of every human life.

It is important to view the image of God properly. Our image-bearing is not dependent on our capacities to think, speak, walk, move, express or any other function. These are all elements of that reflection, but the image of God in any one individual cannot depend on them. There can be no degradation of the image of God, no impact upon the image by our ability to function in any of these ways. For example, if the image required independent movement, then Joni Eareckson Tada has diminished image-bearing, which would fail to pay tribute to the monumental impact her life has had for the gospel.

As we look at our children or friends with disabilities, we view them as distinct image-bearers. We should see them as a means of God's working in this world for his glory, your good, and the good of others with disabilities. This understanding of *imago Dei* gives us a view of Eli as an image-bearer of God, one who has a specific purpose and who will be provided for in that purpose by a loving Father who gives freely and kindly.

## *Growing from Image Bearer to Gospel Messenger*

Our son has shown repentance and faith in Christ alone for his salvation. As a Christian he has a purpose for the sake of the gospel of Jesus Christ. A central focus of the Christian is that they are now a part of the body of Christ (1 Corinthians 12:13–27). Christ's body is the physical representation of Christ assembled to proclaim the gospel through care for one another. Think back to *imago Dei*. If there is no degradation of the image of God as such, then there is no degradation in the role of a member of the body of Christ who has a disability. Namely, they promote the gospel of Jesus Christ.

Eli's life has created a tremendous and eternal impact, even if we just look at his life's shaping effect upon our family. His presence in Ukraine has created access to families; it has changed perspectives on disability; and it has helped others understand the imprint of God upon those with disabilities. When people are in relationship with Eli they are so positively impacted by his love for Jesus. Eli is a blood-bought image-bearer of God and has been called, as all Christians are, to advance the gospel to all nations in keeping with the Great Commission (Matthew 28:18–20).

## *Always Believing That Jesus Is Ultimate*

Disability brings with it a diverse range of needs. Some disabilities require intensive medical care, some require focused therapeutic regimens, and others both medical and therapeutic care. It is not uncommon for the parent of a child with special needs to have a team of specialists to attend to the individual aspects of treatment for their child—physical therapist, occupational therapist, speech therapist, behavioural therapist—and the list goes on. Christians must remember that even these specialists are an expression of God's grace to them through Christ. However, hope is never to be placed in these resources, but only in Christ our eternal hope. Having experienced the many life-enhancing resources that are available in America, we have seen how easy it is to slip into allowing them to become an idol in which we place our hope for our children. It would not be good to focus all one's energy on amassing resources for your child to the exclusion of your other children, your spouse, or your walk with Christ. The hope of a believing parent raising a child with special needs is to be in Christ alone, while giving him glory for the physical or therapeutic resources he so graciously provides.

Resource abundance or resource lack is ultimately dispensed by our good and loving God. Jesus is the ultimate resource manager. Jesus is the ultimate advocate. The Gospels (Mark 9:14–29; John 5; 9) show over and over again just how Christ's heart is tuned to those in need, those who suffer or are on the fringe of society. God the Father's view towards justice and mercy is clearly evident in the Psalms (82:3–4) and Isaiah (Isaiah 30:18–19). He hates oppression, he loves the orphan and widow, he has compassion for those who struggle. God's justice and mercy towards his children in need is clear and generous.

The redemptive thread throughout Scripture is that of a loving and gracious God plucking us out of our sin disability and giving us new life (Ezekiel 36:25–28; John 7:38; 2 Corinthians 4:6; Ephesians 1:18). Quoting all of 1 John would be an appropriate way to express the fullness of God's love for us in Christ. His love is infinite, intimate and immutable. Jesus' love for my child is immutable; it will not change. There is no resource for Eli or care for him that is not issued from the hand of God in perfect love and care. We have witnessed the Lord's affection for our son time and time again, sometimes in big ways but often in small yet consistent means. Eli has experienced much grace. God has cared so lovingly for him throughout his life and he will not stop caring for him. No matter what Eli's future needs, no matter what distance from home, he is not outside the care of his ultimate provider and resource manager . . . Jesus.

### *Making Eli a Participant, Not Just a Recipient*

The gifts of the Spirit are not dependent on being able-bodied or healthy! Bible passages (1 Corinthians 12:18–27; Romans 12:1–8) show no exception clauses that stipulate wholeness or ability in order to be a part of, or serve in, the body of Christ. This is crucial to understanding our brothers and sisters in Christ who have disabilities. They have an equal and perhaps even greater role to play in using their gifts to serve the body (1 Corinthians 12:22).

Eli was created to be a participant in the life of our local church. A couple of years before heading to Ukraine, Calvin, the worship pastor at our church, developed a friendship with Eli, and in so doing, saw Eli's love for worshipping Christ in song. He asked Eli to be a part of the music team for Sunday morning service. We were a bit nervous about the whole idea, but Calvin insisted. Eli was being recognized as an active participant in the body of Christ, not only as a recipient of mercy and compassion from others in the body. His first Sunday on the team arrived and we stood anxiously while he played the 'shaker' with off-beat fervour and joy. Immediately after that service, and many times over the next two years, people came to us in tears telling of how Eli's presence on the stage served to redirect their hearts from a posture of going through the motions to engaging more fully in worshipping our God. We were humbled by the Lord's grace to and through Eli.

Beholding the beauty of someone with a disability, or the 'weaker,' being lovingly pursued for serving the body was truly humbling, but also, as a parent, life-giving. God received the glory, Christ was exalted and a church member with special needs was able to worshipfully serve. Our son was given the opportunity to participate in the body of Christ as a functioning member. Eli's participation in the body of Christ in the Ukrainian context, whilst it might look different, is equally necessary both for his growth and for the unity of the body.

## *Mission Calling Is Family and Individual*

Prior to our departure for Ukraine, our church held a 'sending service' to bless us as we went, and to covenant with us to care for our needs. Our dear friend John Knight preached that evening both to encourage us and remind the church of her responsibility to care for our family and ministry. His teaching contained great insight. Towards the end of his sermon he addressed our family and gave a specific charge to each one of us. He went down the line from me to Tamara and through all five kids, but my eyes flowed rivers of joyful tears as he specifically addressed Eli:

> Elisha, we know God made you just as he intended. Ephesians 2:10 couldn't be more clear: 'for we are his workmanship, created in Christ Jesus for good works, which God prepared beforehand, that we should

walk in them' (ESV). You are his workmanship, Eli. Created for good works. And just to be crystal clear to everyone that it includes Down syndrome, God gave us this, 'Then the LORD said to him, "Who has made man's mouth? Who makes him mute, or deaf, or seeing, or blind? Is it not I, the LORD?"' (Exodus 4:11 ESV). God is delighted in how he made you for his glory, Eli. Don't ever forget that. His glory, his glory and your good!

Eli and John have a friendship that goes back several years. They are two of the most joyful people I know. When John addressed him, Eli sat forward, focused with serious intent on what John was saying to him. It was an altogether serious moment and one with gravity for our family. Eli has a purpose for kingdom advancing ministry with our family in Ukraine. John's words reminded us all, including our five children, that each of us individually were missionaries sent with gospel purpose. We are a missionary family but with individual, God-glorifying purposes.

Biblical thinking is often difficult when approaching a situation such as moving your family, including a disabled child, to a far-away land that rejects people just like him. But God is rich in mercy. He created us in his image for his glory. He caused us to be born again (1 Peter 1:5–7) to a living hope. He provides all that we need unequivocally, in giving us Jesus: we have the ultimate resource for all of life. He moved upon our family to spread his gospel message and, in so doing, is purposeful in each family member's role for his glory and their good.

## Sending Church or Agency Attitudes

Why send a person with a disability on mission? *Imago Dei* establishes the distinct personhood of every human being. Eli is a person, not a disability. He is not identified as a disability. He *has* Down syndrome rather than the common reference that 'he *is* a Down boy.' His personhood comes first and well before any other attribute. Persons have a host of traits that make up who they are, from emotional expression to physical traits, from abilities to gifting. As people who embrace a gospel view of disability, we must be careful about our questioning of the missional ability of a friend with a disability and their fitness for ministry.

In the discernment process, careful inquiry into the life of a person with disability is necessary, but must focus on the work of God in their lives first. We must ask, 'How can we involve this brother or sister in the work of the gospel?' Asking 'why' instead of 'how' can undermine their gifting. These giftings are how the Spirit manifests his power through them as Christians. Asking the question 'why?' can also fall short of loving expectations.

If a typically developing, believing person was 'called' to go into missions, the questions would be different. Because this brother or sister does not have a disability we have different expectations. We have the expectation that their gifting and qualities will serve to advance the gospel. This basic expectation is unquestioned and assumes a certain level of ability to function 'normally.' While this is a safe assumption, are we, by default, developing our expectations out of a utilitarian perspective—that what our brother or sister has to offer physically or mentally determines their worthiness or usefulness to Christ's mission or the Great Commission? The gospel lens gives the surest understanding of our calling into mission. How do you see Christ at work in that person in spite of physical, cognitive, or developmental challenges? They are image-bearers first and, through faith in Christ alone, they are gospel messengers. Can a sovereign, loving God who has made us in his image resource a Christian with disability to go on mission? Resoundingly, yes! Christian love would dictate that believers need to be supported where they can best exercise their gifts as given by God through the Holy Spirit. Perhaps a believer with a disability being in a place absent of a 'disabled' expression of Christianity is the most important work he or she could do.

'Will you take Eli with you?' were often the first words that hung in the air as we began to tell people close to us that we would be transitioning to disability outreach ministry in Ukraine. To this point we had served families experiencing disability and churches seeking to help them for eleven years. Though we could understand why this question came up, we laboured over how to answer it adequately, in a way that pointed to Eli's value to gospel endeavours. We focused on Eli's gifting by the Holy Spirit as giving him a role in the Great Commission, rather than focusing first and solely on his disability. Making these distinctions proved challenging, and at times we would walk away from these conversations battling discouragement and hurt. However, in God's providence, this allowed us to deepen our biblical understanding of Eli's image-bearing of Christ.

## Making Sacrifices and Developing Wise Strategies

Sacrifice is required, and an expected result of the Christian's call to worship with all that we are, even our very bodies (Romans 12:1; Ephesians 5:2). Our understanding of sacrifice is framed biblically by the ultimate sacrifice of

Christ on the cross (John 19). An honest evaluation of what will be required of each family member when heading to a new culture is vital to gaining greater understanding of what sacrifices might need to be made.

We may define sacrifice differently. What might be sacrifice for me may not be sacrifice for you; what is sacrifice for our children may not be sacrifice for a parent. But acknowledging areas of sacrifice helps us to see potential weaknesses, which, in turn, leads us to receive God's grace in that weakness—counselling, need of respite, and more. We could see that for Eli the move would involve sacrifice in terms of three primary areas: access to disability services, loss of relationships and, importantly, losing his role of serving in church. In advance of going we sought to develop specific strategies to prepare for each of these, at least to some degree.

### *1. Finding Appropriate Services in a Resource-Poor Setting*

Taking your child with special needs out of a culture that provides some of the best disability-related resources in the world and moving them to a country with nearly none of these resources requires a creative approach. As parents we know exactly what needs our children have. We know what therapeutic or educational assistance best suits them. Day in and day out we walk through their struggles and victories with them. Eli needs social interaction, special education and speech therapy. Though we can provide some help in these areas, we needed extra help.

Finding a local special educator was key to Eli's support 'team' for our work in Ukraine. Years of partnership with other disability ministries and organizations, along with a lengthy connection with a Christian university, gave us a deep well of resources to draw upon when needed. God providentially brought a couple, one of whom was a special educator! This not only provided educational help to Eli but also provided much-needed help in our ministry. This couple committed to serve with us in Ukraine as educational tutors to the missionary children and to focus on continued educational and life-skills development for Eli.

### *2. Creating Community for Eli in Ukraine*

Social and relational depth for children with special needs is so vital to their lives. In the USA Eli had been a part of a remarkable community of peers, some with special needs and some without, and we knew that losing this network would be the most difficult part of the transition. We would be a part of a new community, a new church family, a new culture, a foreign language and new friends. Developing a new community can be difficult with a new culture and often even more so for people with disability. This unfamiliarity makes transitioning into a new community difficult.

Tamara and I began to feel a tremendous burden for Eli, now a young man, and his need for community in Ukraine. In the USA, we planned to maintain a supportive sending community for our family, and particularly for Eli. In the transition, a continued relationship with our sending church in the USA was important. With the modern marvel of video calls, this has complemented the 'team' that Eli needed for his spiritual development.

But our hope was for the body of Christ to be his community in Ukraine. He came to love youth group and being with friends at our new church in Ukraine; however, as those friends moved on to college he began to lose his community within the church. But God, who is rich in mercy and grace, surrounded Eli with new friends in Ukraine, Christian men who loved him and sought to enable him to serve the body.

### *3. Creating Opportunities for Eli to Serve*

Finally, seeing Eli actively serving the body of Christ in the USA had been one of the greatest joys in our lives, and we hoped that Eli would have an opportunity to serve in the church in Ukraine also. In the USA fellow church members would find Eli and share their appreciation for his service to the church. Often Tamara and I were taken aside by people who expressed through tear-filled eyes how much Eli's simple role in our church music was a reminder to them of the character of our God. Why would we take him away from this special opportunity he had to serve the Lord and the church? This question was difficult and caused us great strain and pleading with the Lord in prayer.

For most of our fellow church members in Ukraine, Eli's presence in church provides their first interaction with disability. That in itself begins to break down barriers in their cultural thinking. Over time these friends have begun to participate in various disability-related outreaches. Some have become passionate about serving the needs of their fellow Ukrainians living with disabilities. Eli's serving, for now, is simply his joyful and worshipful presence in our congregation. He attends outreaches to families experiencing disability and to special needs institutions as well, but his primary service is in faithful church attendance. We are thankful for the Lord's continued grace to Eli and for using him for his glory within our church as people accept and befriend him.

## God's Providence and Provision

We entered Ukraine with nervous anticipation of what the Lord would certainly do, but also of what lay ahead for our family. Despite thorough planning, unexpected things come along that shake us and shape us. Early in 2018 we returned to America for six months to seek better medical intervention for Eli's sister, Naomi. After several weeks of doctor appointments and associated tests we gained clarity on the true diagnosis, Conversion Disorder. Complexity marks this diagnosis and uncertainty of time frame brings a weight to our hearts. With all the focus on Eli and his disability and expecting that his care would be our greatest challenge, we are now faced with the unexpected medical issues of a formerly 'healthy' child. We believe that God is sovereign, we believe that he is purposeful in all things, yet we battle against the heart-crushing agony of our child's struggle and the purpose for her in this difficulty. It is God's providence. This light and momentary affliction faced by Naomi is provided by God for her good, our good, God's glory, and for the sake of the gospel.

We run to the strong tower (Proverbs 18:10), as it is our only refuge against the forces of darkness seeking to vanquish our confidence in Christ. The lessons we have learned in discerning Eli's mission—for example about *Imago Dei*, our ultimate Christ, our calling and our being gospel messengers in suffering—we now need to relearn in the face of Naomi's struggles. What will God in Christ be pleased to do in providing this opportunity? We don't know! But we do know that our Provider gives us all that we need.

Today, the unknown frustrates our desire to act decisively, and to conceive the best possible solution that will put our child in an optimal place of being made well, while also allowing us to continue our mission overseas. Prayer now revolves around waiting on the Lord while learning to trust him and his perfect timing (Psalm 25). We are experiencing a sweetness of grace in the midst of hardship that we know is God's providence. We trust that the sacrifices we have made are for our good, for our children's good and for the glory of Christ.

## Questions, Frustrations and Opportunities

It is understandable, and indeed helpful, to explore the motives, means and methods of those heading into overseas ministry, whether they have a disability or not. Taking Eli's needs into account was an important aspect of our preparation from the outset, as we pursued biblical reasoning and practical considerations.

But questions that focused on Eli's limitations seemed to chip away at his dignity and ability. Eli is an image-bearer, a gospel messenger, who through his faith in Christ is called, Spirit-empowered and gifted for the sake of the body and advancement of the gospel. He is a worthy messenger of the gospel of Jesus Christ and an infinitely valuable part of the body of Christ. His abilities or limitations do not affect his worth in God's eyes, nor should they in ours.

When we met frustration at our decision, we questioned ourselves and we questioned the Lord. Yet at each of these turns the Lord faithfully brought us to our knees in prayer, with our Bibles as our guide, confirming and affirming our next steps (Psalm 37). Wrestling with these issues was not all difficulty. There was much joy and excitement about the open doors before us that we would soon step through for the next stage of life and ministry. We are aware of the unfortunate rarity of taking a child with special needs to an overseas mission field. It is not common and it should be considered with great carefulness and intention. But it should not be so quickly rejected.

Where would we be without pioneering Christians? Church history is filled with scores of people throwing cultural caution to the wind in order to fulfill the Great Commission in reaching the unreached. John Patton lost nearly everything in his efforts to expand the gospel in the New Hebrides islands. Amy Carmichael lived her last twenty years of life in India bedridden by illness, yet she pressed on. What if a teenage girl named Joni had contented herself to simply stay in the background of a truly difficult life of quadriplegia, waiting for healing instead of radically exemplifying faithfulness to her God in spreading the gospel through the influence God gave her? Right actions are often the hardest actions to take. We must not look at difficulty or suffering as end-all answers but as open door opportunities for the glorious gospel of Christ.

## Conclusion

If modern missions and the church continue to delay in engaging people with disabilities for the task assigned to us in the Great Commission, then who will do it? A poorly thought out ideology of many churches views our brothers and sisters with disabilities as simply those who need to be cared for, as though they are eternal children, and thus non-contributors. The secular disability rights movement has led the way in promoting a social model of disability that goes beyond compassion and charity. Yet a Christian understanding of how God works through the seemingly weak and foolish things of this world should give us even greater expectations of those with disabilities. Weakness and inability mark the vessels that Jesus works with and through (1 Corinthians 1:25–31; 2 Corinthians 1:3–7; 3:1–6), not 'wholeness' and strength. A rich biblical view of a believer with a disability looks at how they can *serve*, not just how they can *be* served. How can we help our friends with special needs to be involved in the Great Commission? That is the question that should be asked.

Life in a foreign country is hard. Having a child in the family with special needs in a culture that does not accept him as human is even harder. Watching the struggle of your child processing the harsh views towards disability is heart-wrenching. But God supplies grace and intimacy with the child that is greater than any obstacle we may face. Our desire is to see the glorious gospel of Jesus Christ proclaimed by his people *to* those with disabilities, and proclaimed *by* those with disabilities. We want to see the 'new song' of God's people (Psalm 67; 96) sung by a host of people of all races and all abilities. What a glorious song that will be when our children with disabilities sing forth perfect notes of praise and worship before the audience of One.

CHAPTER 11

# Mission Possible: The Role of Member Care in Mobilizing Workers with Disabilities

Deanna Richey
Director of Personnel and Member Care
SIM Australia

There is a common misconception in mission that God calls into service only the 'super-spiritual,' the most highly gifted and physically strong. It can reflect the churches whence mission candidates emerge. These churches too often exhibit an elitist mentality that puts only the best on display—those who can sing in perfect pitch, the beautiful, the talented—who minister to those who are perceived as 'less than' in some way. Mission practice that flows from this reflects a similar mentality, and can devalue those whom the church seeks to reach. Having our best on display is considered by many to be 'good for business.' However, ministry is 'God's business,' and God in his wisdom rarely approaches things the way fallen humanity does. One need not look further than Christ himself, who came in the weak form of a babe in a stable, exiled, and 'nothing special.' Consider Isaiah 53:2, believed to be speaking of Jesus: 'For he grew up before him like a young plant, and like a root out of dry ground; he had no form nor majesty that we should look at him, and no beauty that we should desire him' (ESV). Sadly, our mission practice can still fail to fully embrace this model as we seek to take this same Christ to a broken and hurting world.

I wonder if we have the wrong idea of what it truly means to give our best to God. I wonder if mission agencies demonstrate a bit of an 'us and them' mentality—borne out of a sense of superiority rather than camaraderie with those who may be different from ourselves. In 2 Corinthians 12:9 Scripture challenges our tendency to value perceived strength too greatly. It reads: 'But he said to me, "My grace is sufficient for you, for my power is made perfect in weakness." Therefore I will boast all the more gladly about my weaknesses, so that Christ's power may rest on me' (ESV). Paul seemed to indicate that working in our own strength can actually become our Achilles heel by making us conceited. But you may be asking, 'Don't we want our mission workers to be strong, and their endeavours effective and sustainable?' The simple answer is, 'Of course!' but mission is never simple. It is frequently messy and always challenging.

## A Brief History of Mission: God at Work through Danger, Death and Disability

'Had I cared for the comments of people,
I should never have been a missionary.'[1]

C T Studd

A common theme emerges in historical accounts of those now considered 'missionary greats': others worked hard to dissuade those who were willing to go. While concerns are often well-intentioned, they fail to consider the bigger picture. Similarly, people with disability who have an interest in mission are often dissuaded.

In the face of peril and threats, many standing on the sidelines perceived certain risks to be too great. Thankfully, mission workers like Carey, Judson and Studd were not dissuaded from their calling to take Christ to the nations. Their stalwart spirit stood firm against the nay-saying fellow Christians of their time, and it inspired others to rise to the challenge despite the risks involved. Early death was one risk readily accepted by newly forming nineteenth-century missionary societies. It was probably for this reason that the young, strong and preferably single were selected for missionary service. Those who did not fit this ideal were often turned away in the most well-intentioned manner.

During these early mission days, society itself modeled similar thinking in excluding people with disabilities.[2] Early missionary societies had many restrictions on who could serve overseas, and people with disabilities were deemed unfit; such restrictions can remain even today. So the early endeavours were often left to the young and strong, as the most likely to survive the rigours of cross-cultural service.

## The Rise of the Member Care Movement

Many returning workers came home earlier than expected, and often were quite broken—mentally, emotionally, spiritually, relationally and physically. In response, the member care movement expanded dramatically towards the end of the twentieth century, leading to better awareness about caring for members, for worker retention and well-being. However, this fostered an overly cautious attitude in regard to accepting the risks associated with potentially vulnerable people, like those with disability. Psychologists and clinicians advising on the home-side were perhaps reactive and risk-averse, using clinical grounds to reject applicants, or to send home existing mission partners.

As a result of member care developments and research on missionary attrition, comprehensive screening methods evolved to get the 'right' workers to the field, while weeding out those less likely to succeed. Mission agencies began to look more closely at applicants' physical, mental and spiritual health, utilizing tools such as psychometric evaluations and medical reports. While the intention behind these new methods was good, it often had the unfortunate consequence of excluding people deemed risky. Those with a perceived defect or disability that might impede ministry were turned away, seemingly for their own good or for the good of the field team, without agencies stopping to realize the discriminatory nature of this. It was, after all, well-meaning.

Specific areas of focus began to emerge that looked at the growing needs of missionary children, who later became known as 'Third Culture Kids' (TCKs). Many of the famous stalwarts had children who died on the mission field, but by the late 1900s this loss of children was considered untenable. The overarching concern for children extended to those whom mission agencies felt might be harmed by being placed at an educational or developmental disadvantage. Under such risk-averse member care practice, children with disability were often an automatic disqualification for a family wanting to serve cross-culturally. The question would be asked, almost rhetorically, 'How could a family adequately care for children with disability while abroad?'

In the last thirty years, there has been a burgeoning array of books, programs, courses and special interest support groups aimed at improving mission practice for worker well-being. We must ask, 'What does this mean for people with mental health issues and disabilities?' Unfortunately, it seems that member care tools and processes were applied more to exclude than facilitate.

## The Lofty 'Ideal'

The lofty idea of the 'ideal missionary candidate' has begun to soften with the reality of the brokenness and complexity of modern society, from which the global missionary workforce arises.

Many of those who approach agencies now come with weaknesses such as physical illness (e.g., food allergies), mental health issues and relational dysfunction. Things that would have prevented workers in times past are now more common. Strikingly, the prevalence of disability in countries like Australia is estimated at 18.3 percent.[3] In my experience, however, mission policies and practices still seem unwilling to look past a perceived risk and fully embrace workers with disabilities. Such cases are often put in the 'too hard' basket with apologies. There is a near absence within the member care literature regarding the management of those with disabilities. However, with appropriate application of modern member care practice, there is hope for change as we continue to move forward.

In mission the complexity can be even greater when it comes to disability inclusion. Member care workers and mission mobilisers need to be equipped to provide direction and advocacy for those who face greater challenges on their missionary journey. It is our role to empower those with disability to answer the calling God has placed upon their lives. There will be times when we seek to find creative placements that provide necessary requirements (e.g., medical and support services); at other times the placement may need to be delayed until the worker's needs can be best met (e.g., team capacity). There will also be times when the best answer for the individual and/or family will be a no. We will explore this in the next section.

## Characteristics of Sustainability

I began my career in church pastoral ministry alongside my husband in the early 1990s in Florida, USA. One family at our church with children of similar ages to ours was looking into the possibility of home missions—their youngest child was on the autism spectrum. We watched as they began the arduous task of what was then known as deputation (partner development for raising support). After many long months and much frustration, they gave up. This was largely because of the cold reception from churches they had visited across North America who misinterpreted behaviours associated with autism. In the early 1990s, there was not a wide understanding of autism, so ultimately their ability to parent was being called into question. Watching our friends go through this process raised many questions in my mind that would resurface years later as God called our family across the ocean to church-planting in Australia.

As I write, my role in ministry has changed. Our own missionary journey was marked by unexpected challenges, as missionary journeys so often are, and these challenges grew in me a desire to see improved mission practice. Counselling studies, which led to an MA in member care, helped me to understand at a deeper level the specific challenges missionaries face across the spectrum of global mission.

Now serving as the Director of Personnel and Member Care for SIM Australia, I have met and worked with many families, some with a disability, as they prepare to serve overseas. It is my job to help prepare them before they go, guide the process of finding the right placements, and track with them as they serve. This is not always easy, and it requires much prayer for wisdom and discernment. We have access to quality research and tools that were not available in centuries past, but it does not come in a 'one size fits all' model for application. Neither is it comprehensive. The world is constantly changing and mission practice needs to change to meet new challenges. The reality is that mission is messy.

While I was completing member care studies, I searched for information on caring for missionary families with children with disability and in particular those with autism spectrum disorders (ASD). Partly, I was driven by memories of my friends' failed dream, but others with similar experiences were crossing my path too. I discovered that there was very little information on sending or supporting mission families with disability. I decided to undertake a small qualitative study of missionary families across agencies to rectify this, hearing their stories and suggestions. Then I worked to merge the literature on member care with best practice support for families living with disability.

My primary focus was ASD, but other developmental disorders were included, with shared similar characteristics and outcomes (increased parental stress, medical needs, etc.). I wanted to understand if we were doing the right thing in mobilizing families with special needs, and if so, what unique support would aid them. The research captured the voices of eleven families and one individual who had walked the missionary road with disability. These families, from the USA, Australia, Great Britain and South Africa, ranged in size from three to six members. Seven families were serving across Africa, two in Europe and two in Asia, in both rural and urban settings. Their length of service ranged from five months to twenty years. The disabilities varied from mild to severe and fell within the classification of neurodevelopmental disorders. These included autism spectrum disorders (ASD), pervasive developmental disorders not otherwise specified (PDD-NOS), profound global developmental delay and articulatory dyspraxia. The data provided information on what went right, what went wrong, and what they thought could be done to improve outcomes for missionaries with disability. It was a rewarding experience for me as a researcher. The families I met and interacted with were inspirational in their passion and enduring strength.

Families with disability tended to share similar struggles. Perhaps most significant was the struggle for understanding and acceptance from churches and fellow teammates. Often, when these families needed the support most, they were sent home with a sense of rejection. This left a long-term impact, especially when workable solutions to enable them to stay (or return to the field) were not explored. Shared feelings of grief were common among these families, who were already grieving during the time leading up to and shortly after diagnosis. I met one family seven years after their return home. Their field team had waited until after they had begun their home assignment to ask them to not return. The lack of opportunity to say proper goodbyes on the field was devastating to their two sons on the autism spectrum.

Many with special challenges are equipped with a special strength firmly in place. The families I interviewed had each learned similar lessons as they navigated medical and social support structures, both in their country of origin and on the field. They worked hard to advocate for their children, helping them to adjust and adapt in a foreign setting where change was frequent, and many exceeded their own expectations. Faith grew deeper and they grew stronger with a determination to make things work, even though the challenges were many. And when things didn't work as they hoped, they found alternate means to fulfil the calling God had placed on their life. This is known as resilience, and it is a highly sought-after character quality of mission workers from all walks of life. This resilience seems to be a by-product of facing daily challenges when overcoming disability as an individual or a family.

Much research has been devoted in recent years to understanding the concept of resilience. It is the ability to return to equilibrium or bounce back after being pressed or crushed. The end result often yields what has come to be known as 'post-traumatic growth.' A similar idea is hinted at in 1 Peter 5:10. Those who have successfully navigated their disability diagnoses and found new norms have a proven strength that serves them and others well amid the challenges of mission. This overcoming spirit can inspire others who have struggles to see that they too can overcome.

Overcoming disadvantage enables missionaries to model to those among whom they minister how to rise above their own challenges of poverty, abuse, marginalization and even disability. Disability-inclusive missionary teams can make a much broader and deeper impact than those perceived as advantaged workers from the West. One inspirational example comes from our own team of senders in Australia, Andrew.

After collapsing from a brain tumor while serving in West Africa, and following many surgeries and treatments which left significant impairments, Andrew continued to help prepare new workers going overseas. Additionally, he and his family maintain regular contact with their West African friends, offering mentoring and ongoing encouragement from afar. Their testimony of patient endurance, strength and reliance on God in the trials of life makes them easy to relate to. Having moved from a perceived position of 'entitled Western missionary,' they now live out the example of how faith works in life's hard realities. This is inspirational for their West African friends, who now join in prayer for the challenges faced by this family. This is how mutuality and equality in mission should work—all are valuable and have something to offer to one another. This family has been a valuable asset to our team in so many ways!

## Member Care Responses to Stressful Realities

We need to acknowledge the difficulties of being a missionary overseas. Stress research by the mental health sector estimates that the average missionary worker sits at a significantly higher-than-normal sustained stress level, placing them at greater risk for mental, emotional, physical and relational health breakdown. This is due to several factors: for example, frequent transition, language learning, cultural acquisition, sustained cross-cultural living, increased security threats against foreigners, poor living conditions that frequently pose health risks, spiritual warfare, grief from multiple ongoing good-byes, minimal support networks, financial strain and team dysfunction. Disability comes with its own set of unique stresses that could compound the already high baseline. It is wise member care practice to monitor risk and implement early interventions to keep workers healthy and on mission.

We want workers to do what they have been called by God to accomplish. Families with disability may need extra counselling services, educational services for children with special needs and (especially) specific and intentional prayer. Modern technology has improved our access to workers, and the workers' access to a wider and more integrated network of care, which includes church, agency, supporters and helping professionals who live on a different continent. In some ways, it is like Moses on the mountaintop with the battle raging below. Others came beside him to hold up his arms when he began to grow weary (Exodus 17:12–14). The cooperative effort through a network of carers can improve worker wellbeing dramatically, and is essential in helping people with disability to remain in service.

We all have needs, and that is one reason that working in Christian community is vital. My research in the area of ASD showed the importance of understanding the challenges of managing this disability. This was key to knowing how best to facilitate the sending and support of these families. But understanding is often missing or grossly limited. Workers in developing countries feel additional stress when disabilities are perceived to be a spiritual issue. There is evidence from the recent past that this was happening in the West as well.[4] Intentional, ongoing education within society has helped to rectify these misconceptions, but more work is needed.

Families with a child with disability were able to serve for longer if placed in a situation where routines could be established. This allowed them to build strong supportive relationships with teams that themselves had stable and strong support networks. One excellent arena for this type of placement was in international or missionary schools. These schools are generally located in urban centres, which usually have greater access to support services such as psychologists, speech therapists and occupational therapists, as well as medical doctors. Generally, member care should seek to place those families into well-functioning teams that have capacity to be supportive and welcoming. Our systems do sometimes fail us. I think of one family in a well-resourced area of the world whose child was asked not to return to school due to a lack of skilled teaching staff. This highlights the need for agencies to work harder to mobilize disability support personnel, to increase the capacity of under-resourced teams.

We must also work with mission teams to increase their willingness to have people with disability serving with them. I recall a comment made at a personnel conference that I have heard many times in other arenas, 'Please don't send us needy workers!' This was not directed towards any particular people or group, but reflected that teams feel they lack capacity to give extra support. Typically, this is in reference to workers who are perceived as emotionally needy. I always find this interesting in the sense that every new missionary worker is 'needy' in the beginning until they have had a chance to gain some level of cultural proficiency. This can take years! The problem of teams being stretched too thin happens frequently. While people and families with disability are not necessarily needy, there could be a perception of increased neediness. Sending agencies should work closely in support of the field team to choose appropriate fields when placing people with disability.

The field of service needs to be carefully and prayerfully thought through when considering a person with disability, as it does when placing a person without disability. Some more established fields will likely have well-developed infrastructure and field-based resources (e.g., well-established schools with special needs teachers). Some fields are more difficult places to live than others, whether through inhospitable terrain, isolation from services, or war and terrorism targeting foreigners. It is becoming more common for member care staff within agencies to visit field teams to better understand their challenges. This insight will help in making decisions on the sending end to find just the right fit for service. Field leadership should be made aware of specific needs prior to mobilization of workers. A thorough assessment of support needs prior to placement should limit frustration upon arrival. This will lead to ministry partnership that is mutually supportive and reasonably safe for all involved. A challenging field environment is not a criterion for excluding people with disability, but does call for a conversation around the specifics of the disability, the family situation and the resilience of the person with disability.

Personality can play a large part in how stress is felt and managed. As in every context, stressed people can be overly self-protective, and lack energy to grapple with the unfamiliar. This means we must work hard to encourage good stress management, with healthy stress-coping outlets for all team members. Stress should be monitored, with adjustments made where possible to reduce negative impact.

Additionally, it became clear through my research how little sending office leadership knew about autism spectrum disorders. This meant that decisions were often made with little information. The more a disability is understood, and the more clearly the needs of the individual or family are made known, the better the risk can be managed. All parties need to educate one another as to the best way forward.

## Mission Possible!

Many mission agencies have been growing their capacity to send workers with special challenges. These may include significant health and dietary restrictions, a history of mental or emotional health disturbance, developmental disabilities and similar things. Adaptability in praxis and flexibility in mind-set help aid this process. In their book, *Serving at the ends of the earth: Family life and TCKs*, Steve and Gill Bryant cover many issues that families face in mission.[5] The Bryants served overseas with a child who had additional challenges, and worked for years in the UK with a multiplicity of families on mission, so they are well placed to help others navigate challenges. In their chapter on children who face disabilities, they list four main areas to be considered: (1) the nature and extent of the disability; (2) the parents' ability to cope; (3) the planned place of service and receiving team; and (4) the suitability of schools and health care in that place. Areas (1) and (3) are relevant for adults with disability as well. This framework is a helpful place to start.

Mission agencies should consider what is known within the disability movement as a 'twin-track approach.' This means providing care for the missionary with disability while creating an inclusive, supportive environment for them in the field.

It requires an individualized approach. Working through this framework will help guide the process for each unique scenario. It should take into account:

### *Individual Level*

1. The person being sent—his or her spiritual readiness, sense of calling and psychological/mental readiness.

2. The family unit, in areas of general coping, shared motivation, unity of purpose (e.g., no trailing spouses), coping capacity and any evidence of stress break in individual family members.

### *Environment*

1. The receiving team. Questions to answer are, 'Is this the best team?' and, 'How do we best help prepare them to receive this family?'

2. The resources available in the country to care for the disability, such as schooling, therapy and accessibility. Ask: Is there a country that better meets the needed criteria?

3. The sending agency, which looks at the practical areas of insurance coverage availability, the potential for a better fit with another agency, or even tent-making non-agency approaches.

The SIM Australia office sent out a second-generation missionary family managing a child with a disability. We were relatively ignorant at the time of important criteria that should have been considered. The context in which they served required regular mobility and lacked sufficient support structures. Ultimately, they returned home after only eighteen months, as it became apparent that the family's well-being was at stake.

They returned to Australia a bit bruised and battered, but not finished. Their short time in the field laid an important base for their long-term work, despite the skepticism of fellow team members. Capitalizing on this foundation, they have been able to provide the entire mission with renewed passion and vision for reaching the 'desert tribes' across parts of Africa and Asia. They have mobilized a considerable amount of prayer for these regions, as well as workers, and we are seeing great results as God answers those prayers. The family is in a much healthier place back in Australia, with needed supports. They play a crucial role in mission, likely bigger than they could have accomplished from the field alone.

Providing support before families go out can reduce the chance of their having to come home like this. There are often creative ways to support workers. For example, a few years ago SIM was approached by a young woman diagnosed with Asperger's syndrome. She had received her diagnosis in her mid-teens after suffering social isolation and bullying from classmates. While this was difficult for her, it motivated her to be an advocate for others who are marginalized. When she first came to us in her twenties, we were a little skeptical about finding the right placement. We knew that support raising could prove challenging for her due to the social strain of addressing church meetings, and we were not sure how she would adapt to picking up cultural cues that would help her adjust to daily living in her host culture. However, her parents were willing to travel with her and even ended up joining her in service overseas. They played the role of 'enablers.' They have now entered into their second term of service running a children's home, and are loving it and doing a terrific job. The relationship she has been able to build with these castaway children is wonderful, for she understands their pain on a deep level, and she loves them with abandon. This is what mission should look like.

One of my well-respected colleagues in member care is psychologist and author Debbie Hawker Lovell. Debbie supports humanitarian aid workers and mission workers around the world, and she has helped train many member care practitioners with her wealth of knowledge and her kind heart. Her work requires a great deal of travel. Debbie recently shared a bit of her story in her book, *The Curious Incident of a Boy's Transformation: Helping a Child on the Autistic Spectrum*.[6]

Debbie, who is based in the UK, travels as much as possible with her husband, David, and son, Pip, both of whom are on the autism spectrum. She notes that travel could prove quite challenging with Pip, but says that Pip adjusts well and enjoys experiencing the different cultures in Africa, Asia, America, Europe and the Middle East. He is, Debbie notes, 'used to it,' and so does not find travel as stressful as some people on the autism spectrum might. Debbie and David help prepare him by giving him details of what to expect. In this way, Pip and the family can manage the stresses that come with new situations. The whole family is an encouragement and inspiration to countless workers around the world, as they are an example of managing mission from a stable home base.

There are many other encouraging examples in this book. More stories can and should be shared for the glory of God. Only God knows what a tremendous kingdom impact these faithful servants have had, and continue to have, for all eternity! As a member care movement we can and should learn from these stories how best to support such families in their journey of serving in missions.

## Inclusiveness—the Way Forward

The early pioneer workers were discouraged from their passion to share Christ for fear of their safety, and sometimes because it seemed a waste of their abilities. I fear that we, with good intentions, can discourage those with the added challenges of disability. Thankfully, that is not always the case, and the member care movement would be wise to learn from history.

Laws have been passed in Western countries only in fairly recent years to protect the rights of those with disabilities in the workplace; we, as a global church, should be leading the way in opening up the mission workplace. It is time we saw this change. The practical suggestions discussed can be summarized as:

- Choose appropriate placements / relocate current workers.
    - Seek to understand the unique challenges facing the family.
    - Consider the optimal context for service (e.g., urban centres, international schools ministry).

   - Provide placement stability that doesn't require regular change.
   - Connect these families to well-functioning teams for support.
- Support the workers with disability in the field.
   - Develop an integrated network of care that links the church, agency, supporters and health professionals.
   - Ensure accessibility to necessary supports and information including counselling services and educational assistance for the child.
   - Ensure there are regular opportunities to debrief.
- Support the sending churches, missions agencies and receiving teams.
   - Challenge any incorrect biblical understandings that might stigmatise disability in mission.
   - Educate them about how to provide support to the person with disability and their family.
   - Dialogue with the field site or team to promote better understanding of the disability and plan potential roles on the field.

The member care movement, and others who support and send missionaries, must be willing to take considered risks, for only then will our mission workforce be complete. With God's help, we are beginning to see changes.

## Further Reading

Bosch, D. *Transforming Mission: Paradigm Shifts in Theology of Mission.* Mary Knoll: Orbis Books, 2011.

Foyle, M. *Overcoming Missionary Stress.* Wheaton: Evangelical Missions Information Service, 1987.

Foyle, M. *Honourably Wounded: Stress among Christian Workers.* Oxford: Monarch Books, 1987.

Hay, R, V Lim, D Blöcher, J Keteaar, and S Hay. *Worth Keeping: Global Perspectives on Best Practice in Missionary Retention.* Pasadena, CA: William Carey Library, 2007.

Lindquist, B. *Bringing Member Care Home: Member Health*? Fresno, CA: Link Care Center, 2008.

O'Donnel, K, and M O'Donnel, eds. *Helping Missionaries Grow: Readings in Mental Health and Mission*, Pasadena, CA: William Carey Library, 1988.

Spruyt, E, and R Schudel. *Biblical Member Care*. Cessy, Fr.: Le Rucher Ministries; Mercy Ministries International, 2012.

Taylor, W, ed. *Too Valuable to Lose: Exploring the Causes and Cures of Missionary Attrition*. Pasadena, CA: William Carey Library, 1997.

CONCLUSION

# Disability and Mission: For His Glory

Nathan G John

God, in his sovereignty, is working through those with disability to reach the nations. Like the disciples in John 9 who ask, 'Who sinned, this man or his parents, that he was born blind?' society often assumes the worst about people with disabilities. They are considered weak. Yet each of the powerful testimonies here affirms how God chooses weak people, equips them powerfully by his grace, and works through them. There is something about disability that enables us to experience a powerful move of God in our lives, our ministry, and our mission.

Disability is a treasure in a dark place. Isaiah 45:3 says 'I will give you hidden treasures, riches stored in secret places, so that you may know that I am the Lord, the God of Israel, who summons you by name.'

Treasure indeed—and eternal treasure—in seeing people experience God's healing; seeing one's quadriplegia bring people to Christ; seeing one's child, born with a profound disability, transforming the life of a young survivor of suicide. I think of Ephesians 3:20—how he is 'able to do immeasurably more than all we ask or imagine, according to his power that is at work within us.' In the various stories we see his power at work in our broken bodies, and the Lord working creatively beyond what we could imagine in our limited minds.

Some chapters may be uncomfortable—for churches and for mission agencies. What we learn from observing disability in missions, and from building a biblical theology of disability, applies to us all. God will work everything together for good, as per his great missional narrative. We need to lay our abilities and disabilities at his feet and allow him to work.

Let me summarise the themes and ideas echoed through these pages.

## The Biblical Mandate to Include People with Disability

The Bible has many examples of God choosing to work through the weak to overcome tremendous odds, and in so doing to reveal his wonderful power. Moses, who has a heavy tongue and slowness of speech, is called to take on Pharaoh, the most powerful ruler of that time. Gideon, whose army is whittled back to just three hundred men, is told to face the mighty Midianites. David, a shepherd boy, is selected to take on a giant. What do these stories share in common?

1. All are weak, seemingly by God's design. They're 'weak-tongued' boys, from the 'weakest clan,' 'least in their father's house.' Unimpressive is their offering. Yet seemingly God has chosen them precisely because they are weak! He even creates us with disability, as God explains in response to Moses' low self-esteem and feelings of inadequacy: 'Who made man weak; was is it not I? Now get on with the job, Moses!' (paraphrased).

2. All face overwhelming odds, which God seems intent on making even worse. All are vastly outnumbered. With no armour, David faces a giant, and Moses the might of Pharaoh's army.

3. God's grace and power are sufficient in his servants' inadequacy and weakness.

4. The battle belongs to the Lord! In the weakness of his servants, God's strength works to bring God all the glory. And that, after all, is the chief end of humanity and the source of our fullest joy!

God called Gideon to deliver his people. Gideon blew trumpets and amassed a mighty army, gathering 32,000 fellow Jews to face 135,000 Midianites. If I had been in his shoes, I would have begged God for more soldiers, as they were outnumbered four to one. What did God do? He reduced their numbers! He told Gideon, 'Your army is too great and capable. You have too many men. There is too much strength. If you win a victory, it might seem that you won it by yourself—strictly by your own abilities. You've got too much going for you. It might rob glory from me. So, reduce your army!' (paraphrase of Judges 7:2–3). Then through a two-step process God whittled the army down to a mere 300 men, on the basis of drinking habits rather than prowess in battle. Gideon must have stood in utter dismay and wondered: How can we win by becoming weaker? He was outnumbered 450 to 1!

God weakens his vessels to work powerfully in them and achieve his plans—as is clearly echoed through this book. Many of the contributors faced overwhelming odds—and often God seems to make things even more overwhelming! In this weakness God fights the battles for his 'weak' missionaries and therefore he gets the glory. We are weak for his glory.

## Disability Makes Us Better Missionaries

'God crushes all our self-dependence and, in its place, substitutes an utter dependence on God and God alone.'[1]
Lon Solomon

Another Bible character of note in the disability space is the apostle Paul. David Deuel refers to him as a missionary of weakness. Nearly all the contributors refer to the life and teachings of Paul on weakness. From jail Paul writes, 'Three times I was beaten with rods, once I was pelted with stones, three times I was shipwrecked' (2 Corinthians 11:25). Then he had a thorn that tormented him. But ultimately God's power (as opposed to Paul's) was made perfect in his weakness.

The purpose of the thorn in Paul's ministry is similar to that of weakness in the ministries of Moses, Gideon and David. It works as a vaccination against pride and conceit! All these men were prone to struggling with pride associated with power. In making his missionaries weak, outnumbered and powerless, God protects them from this. In his treatise on weakness in 2 Corinthians 12, Paul explicitly states that the purpose of his thorn/weakness was to prevent him from becoming conceited (v. 7).

Many stories here follow a similar narrative. Barry Funnell speaks of his conceit being shattered by a fall that left him a paraplegic. In his inadequacy he became dependent on God's grace and power. It's a severe mercy! This was also my experience, wherein disability prevented me from becoming (more) conceited. My life was 'together' by the world's standards: a successful doctor, academic and well-prepared missionary. This togetherness could have become my ultimate meaning (read, idol). That is, until our beautiful daughter came into our world with a gift of profound disability. I realized that if worldly success defines who we are, then my daughter was a failure—a nothing. Yet God had made her someone, someone as beautiful as his image. God has a habit of refining us and bringing us back to him through disability.

If disability keeps us from becoming conceited, it also promotes dependence—on others and, more importantly, on God. Our authors outline how God-dependence (for them, gained through disability) is a vital qualification for ministry and mission. Disability, impairment and weakness lead them to turn to God humbly and acknowledge that apart from him they cannot be on mission.

Bonnie Armistead refers to disability as a disciplining that exposed and dismantled the worldly values she had adopted. Severe mercy came to her in the form of a baby girl with Down syndrome. She describes being in 'complete dependence on God for everything: future provision, plans, guidance, grace.' Barry Funnell, in bed, on his back, now with paraplegia, realises he can do nothing. He is entirely dependent on God, and he turns to his Bible for comfort and encouragement. This once-arrogant, strong and ambitious dental student found his identity in the love of Christ. 'My worth or joy in life does not come from being physically fit and well; it comes from the fact that I am a person loved by God. God's love is also unconditional, which I have mentioned before, and not dependent on whether I can walk or not.' When we are disabled it allows God to be—as Paul Lindoewood describes—our 'enabler,' which shows those we are serving that the surpassing power belongs to God and not to us! Disability is for God's glory.

## Disability Promotes Interdependence

Dependence on God's people, our brothers and sisters, is healthy, as it reminds us that this is not 'my mission' but 'our mission.' This is mission as God intended it; a communal work of the church, or the body. For mission, as indeed all ministry, relies on all parts of the body playing their God-designed role, working towards a common goal.

My wife and I have become dependent on others as we serve in mission whilst living with disability. The concept of the interdependent body of Christ (1 Corinthians 12:12–26) has become a defining Bible truth for our journey. We were well prepared and relatively self-sufficient in going about our mission. We were doctors, 'tent-makers,' and not financially dependent on others. But after our daughter's birth we became completely dependent, just to get through each day. We could not have remained in mission without the very practical support of our church, friends and family. My mother became every bit a missionary; she had felt called to missions as a young woman, yet the pressures of life and four children crowded out any mission endeavour . . . until her son, on the mission field, had a child with profound disability. Now her practical care and help, both on and off the field, allows this mission to continue. In a very practical way, my mother is serving as part of the mission. She was dependent on us for her calling to be realised, and we are dependent on her to continue ours.

So disability makes us acutely aware of our need to apply this biblical model of the body, each dependent on all parts. It is a healthy rebuff to our sinful Western worldview that venerates independence. And that ideal too often flows into the mission mentality whereby, after garnering financial and prayer support, missionaries are in effect independent units, working to achieve what they believe is their call.

Jeff McNair's chapter paints the beautiful scene of a short-term team made up of people with disabilities and people without disabilities. Both groups benefitted. Should this not become a reality for long-term field teams? Often the physical dependence of the person with disability is obvious. But in less obvious ways, as those with disability display their unique gifts, those without disability come to depend on them too. The disability is for God's glory.

## Disability Creates Opportunities to Witness

> 'I dare say the greatest earthly blessing that God can give to any of us is health, *with the exception of sickness . . .*'[2]

The central aim of missions must be sharing the gospel with those who have not heard, leading, by the grace of God, to personal, social and relational transformation. We read stories here of disability providing an avenue for this. Barry Funnell recounts, 'I found people very willing to talk to me about matters of faith. I believe my wheelchair disarmed them. . . . God has used my disability to open hearts to the gospel.' Disability, minor or major, opens a space for deep reflection and sharing.

Missionaries with disability can vividly understand the grief and struggles that others with disability feel. They can share deeply in a place of trust that is unique to them. Our writers here (myself included) were all inspired to work in disability through our own circumstances. Our experience of disability has been our source of up-skilling! Elena Down, to whose memory this book is dedicated, at first tried to disown her disability. By lip-reading, sign language and technology she could function highly, and she graduated as a lawyer. She chose to take her skills to the mission field, but it was only begrudgingly that she accepted her mission agency's request for her to serve amongst the deaf in China. Similar to the witness of each of our authors, her impairment gave her numerous opportunities to share her heart for Jesus! She came to accept that her deafness was a gifting from God. It was part of the unique way that God had created her for his purpose. Sadly, we will need to wait until heaven to learn Elena's full story, as she tragically passed away before she could complete her chapter.

When people see the love we have for those with disability, they ask, 'Why?' In India that question is often asked of those who 'waste' their time caring for a person with disability, a person supposedly cursed by God for sins in a past life, a person with no value. And the answer is clear. Christ tells us to. God loves every soul. Every child of creation was made equal. All have immense value. These answers changed Hadassah's life. J M Paul describes how Hadassah, who has a significant facial deformity from an attempted suicide by immolation, was convicted by the Pauls' love for little Adam, who also had a significant facial deformity. Why would the Pauls care? Because of Christ. And this is what Hadassah now shares with others.

This outreach—motivated and informed by disability—bears on all of us who have experienced weakness, loss, pain and grief. That's everyone! As Bonnie Armistead beautifully explains, 'Shared weakness was like a bridge that connected my heart to theirs, irrespective of race or religion.' Disability can change the perception of a Western missionary from being viewed as a rich, intelligent and powerful foreigner to being viewed as a friend on the same level as the community. When we're face-to-face and eye-to-eye with others, we often come heart-to-heart as well, and we can share the comfort that we have received from Christ. A friend working in Bangladesh explained to me how when people see his deformity it cuts through an unhealthy power dynamic. All of a sudden they see him as a real person at their level, and they open up and share about their own disability or issue. He described to me his encounter with a woman who saw that he had a similar disability to her son, whereupon she spontaneously removed her Burqa headdress to have a closer look. Disability can break down barriers, for God's glory!

## The Reality of the Struggle of Disability and Missions

There is a risk that these stories glorify disability and belittle the pain. The disability rights movement might have us believe that disability is 'good,' and that the problem lies with the environment, which doesn't cater for disability. This is known as the *social model* in the disability sector. I subscribe to and teach on the social model, but this approach should not gloss over the very real element of pain and suffering. We are created with DNA and genes that have been coded for specific functions. It is a real loss when these genes are disrupted, when an accident impedes our function, or when chronic disease robs us of health.

The pain and suffering is very real for each of the contributors to this book, including us, the editors. Throughout Kasonga's ministry in Zambia, he suffered pain and debility as a result of leprosy. And Natalie Flickner vividly explains how she has suffered with cerebral palsy, compounded by a rare genetic condition and then deep depression. The pain is very real. It's not easy to live with a disability, and it's certainly no easier to live with it on the mission field.

Make no mistake. Raising a child with disabilities on the field may be one of the hardest and most time-consuming things a person could ever do. In Bonnie Armistead's words, 'Our journey . . . has been long and arduous, fraught with questions.' We would not ask for this. But there is a paradox at play, as beautifully expressed by Isaiah the prophet, 'I will give you treasures hidden in the darkness—secret riches' (45:3 NLT).

These secret riches were discovered by an unknown battle-weary soldier near the end of the American Civil War.

### "Most Richly Blessed"<br>by an Unknown Civil War Veteran

I asked God for strength, that I might achieve.
I was made weak, that I might learn humbly to obey.
I asked for health, that I might do great things.
I was given infirmity, that I might do better things.
I asked for riches, that I might be happy.
I was given poverty, that I might become wise.
I asked for power, that I might have the praise of men.
I was given weakness, that I might feel the need for God.
I asked for all things, that I might enjoy life.
I was given Life, that I might enjoy all things.
I got nothing that I asked for, but everything I had hoped for.
Almost despite myself, my unspoken prayers and true needs
were fulfilled.
I am, among all men, most richly blessed.

God has purposes, or 'treasures,' in disability, and as such redeems it for his glory. At the same time as experiencing pain we can rejoice in this knowledge. Paul describes this paradox in 2 Corinthians 6:10 in our being 'sorrowful, yet always rejoicing.' The Bible does not teach us to pretend there is no pain, and we are not called to rejoice that we have pain. But we are called to rejoice in God *at the same time*. In the midst of my daughter's disability, and the resultant struggles in our family, I have been able to rejoice in understanding who God is and in seeing how he works. It is for God's glory.

## The Changing Face of World Mission Creates Space for People with Disabilities

The stories in this book illustrate creative ways that people with disability can be involved in missions. Some used their disability to launch into ministry. Others forged creative ways to stay on mission. However, such novel approaches may not fit within traditional mission agency categories. Nor do they necessarily conform to the traditional model of relocating to a low-income country and serving there for many years before their first home assignment.

Excitingly, we are now seeing the evolution of the mission movement where alternative and non-traditional approaches are becoming the norm. This environment is one where people with disability can be creatively included.

I hope that these chapters may prompt agencies and churches to consider new ways of engaging those we have sometimes rejected. Are we ready? Perhaps a more relevant question is: Can we afford not to do so? We can't afford to recruit only 'ideal' missionaries, if they actually even exist.

There are many ways to measure the prevalence of disability, and a range of surveys covering mental and physical aspects. At the most conservative estimate 18.3 percent of Australians have disabilities.[3] We cannot afford to exclude people on the basis of disability when so few are prepared to answer God's call to mission. This was so even in the era of Hudson Taylor in the nineteenth century. George Stott (1835–1889), a one-legged school teacher from Scotland, approached Hudson Taylor offering himself for service in China. Hudson Taylor asked, 'With only one leg, why do you think of going as a missionary?' Stott replied, 'I do not see those with two legs going, so I must.' Stott was accepted and served in China for twenty-four years, becoming the first missionary to Wenzhou province, and a highly effective mission leader.[4]

In the twenty-first century, where is the mission field? Unreached people do not necessarily live in poor countries, where it might be dangerous for a person with disability. Japan is surely no riskier to people with disability, in terms of access to therapy and rehabilitation, than their own country. The same or even better services would be available in Japan. This challenges some traditional arguments against sending people with disability. Poor access to disability services can no longer be the sole reason for a mission agency not sending a person with disability. Of course, the issue, as Paul Lindoewood comments, might have a bearing on financial resources required.

Missions can now involve living remotely so the person with disability has access to the required services. There is no longer an absolute requirement for a missionary to be based full-time in a specific country. There are part-time and serial short-terming options, and in between trips there can be low-cost communication. I have been involved in mission in India since 2004 but, due to our daughter's needs, I have averaged only three months per year in country. Yet, I speak daily with my staff in the field, at virtually no cost, perhaps talking more with them than I would if I were living in country.

These creative models allow more people to serve, and also provide a halfway house for wounded missionaries. Adaptive flexible models of mission service avoid the need to either fight to the death or return for good. Maybe relocating to an environment in a more developed city nearby is an option. For example, Barry Funnell, translating the Bible in a remote village in rural Africa, moved to a nearby city that better accommodated his physical limitations. He continued serving there for many years. For me, the strategic retreat has meant withdrawing to our sending country and making short trips from there. Disability no longer disqualifies missionaries, but it may mean doing mission differently.

This changing face of modern missions requires that sending churches and agencies rethink how they assess potential missionaries. Many of the missionaries in these chapters would have been rejected due to their disability if they were to apply to their mission agency today! Of course, a disability could well mean that one does not go to the mission field (or returns sooner), but equally, God doesn't intend to exclude people from missions merely because they experience disability. A recurring theme in this book is that we need to be careful not to unthinkingly apply the world's values and criteria for success when selecting missionaries.

Instead we need to consider how we can undertake missionary endeavours creatively as we select the location, utilize technology and plan carefully. This allows Christians, whatever their vulnerability, to use their gifts in imaginative ways for God's glory.

## 'Enablement' of People with Disability in Ministry

Whilst disability does not preclude mission, it does require careful management of the environment to enable those with disability to serve. The World Health Organization defines disability as an outcome of the interaction between impairment and the environment in which people live.[5] This puts the onus on society, or an employer, or even the receiving mission field, to match a person to an accessible place, and/or to make the environment as accommodating as possible.

Indeed, if it were in the USA, Australia or Europe, then by law the employer would be required to ensure the workplace be as inclusive as possible. Whilst there is a clear limitation in how much of the mission environment we can modify, we should be encouraging sending agencies and the field receiving sites not to ask 'How could X disabled person possibly cope?' but rather, 'How can we make adjustments to the field, or choose the right field, so they can thrive?' If we do not do this, then by the World Health Organization's definition, we may be disabling potential missionaries who have impairments.

The mission movement should focus more on how to enable those with disability to serve, and to continue serving. Deanna Richey encourages agencies to be more willing to consider candidates with disability, whilst not suggesting that all be accepted. She advocates a 'twin-track approach' to maximise the person's gifts by ensuring supports are in place and barriers are removed (environment). At its simplest, this could mean taking into account the individual's characteristics and finding a supportive field site.

A supportive field site does not just mean the physical environment. The care network—including family, church and colleagues—is key in enabling those with disability and their families to serve in mission. Those around the person with weakness or disability can play an enabling role just as Aaron was the enabler of Moses in the mission God gave to Moses. Richey tells a powerful story about a young woman with autism spectrum disorder who felt called to the mission field. Her parents accompanied her to the field to support her calling. What a story of enablement! Likewise, Bonnie Armistead identifies her role as an enabler 'to facilitate [Anna] developing to her fullest potential, but also to harvest the fruit that the Lord wants to bring forth in Indonesian hearts as a result of her ministry.'

One particularly important area to enable families with a child with disability to serve is careful planning around education. Children's education, or children not integrating well in the field, is the most common reason, apart from retirement, that missionaries return home.[6] And this is even more pertinent for families with special needs. What comes through in Bonnie Armistead's chapter is the importance of providing educational options and educational supports for children with disability on the field. She references a Christian community that worked with them to provide for Anna's educational needs. That is, the Christian school adapted their educational environment, which in turn allowed Anna to stay at school, and her parents to remain on the field.

## Supporting the Call of God

The single factor that stands out in this book is a strong sense of calling. This was common for the authors who served in mission despite disability. For example, for the Armisteads, a sense of calling to Indonesia led them to pursue options to remain on the field when it would have been all too easy—and completely acceptable to friends, family and church—to return home to the United States. However, their overwhelming sense of calling, and God's grace, kept them on mission. Doing mission is hard. Doing mission in the context of disability is even harder. But if we clearly know God wants us on that mission, then we are prepared to walk that hard path for his glory.

The agency is called to support those who are called. The agency should not be seen as a panel to weed out people who are not perfect. Instead the agency needs to walk beside the person/family with disability in exploring their calling. We need to think creatively in selecting and creating a supportive environment. We need to help strengthen the circles of care both at home and in the field. If God is calling an individual or family to serve in mission, we need to consider all possible means to enable them to do so, for his glory.

## Conclusion: Including the Treasures of the Church in Mission

God has called all of us to be involved in mission in some way, with or without disability. If we are interested in taking our impairment out to the mission field, we should be assured that this is consistent with biblical history and God's imagination.

Maybe we feel disability and other vulnerabilities make us too weak to be on mission. We question if we really have the 'ability' to serve God in mission.

Remember that the odds against us could be there by God's design to allow his strength to work through our weakness. Otherwise, when he gives fruit in ministry, we might claim glory for ourselves, believing 'My own hand has done this' (see Judges 7:2).

In his sovereignty, God seems to take pleasure in working through our disability and our inadequacy. Our weakness is his strength! In his upside-down kingdom, God may intend to work through our weakness more than our strength. Indeed, disability, weakness and even brokenness are perhaps qualifications for mission!

To be effective, the mission movement needs every part of the body of Christ 'on mission.' If we do exclude people with disability from missions, then the mission movement is missing part of the body. The mission is itself disabled. And that's not God's plan.

These stories of God working through disability aren't isolated examples. We have come across many similar stories whilst writing this book, such as Elinor Young's story of how her 'Bad Legs' were a symbol to an unreached people group in West Papua of just how much God loved them.[7]

We hope this book will encourage others to share their stories and continue this important conversation, which in turn would see others with disabilities involved in missions.

People with disability can be enabled in mission through care, support and acknowledgement of their gifts. People with disability can be the treasures of the church and mission movement. This will bring God greater glory.

# Contributors

**Bonnie Armistead** was serving among a UPG in Southeast Asia when the Lord took her on a side journey into the world of disability. Though she holds a BA in political science from the American University in Washington, DC, and an MDiv from Gordon-Conwell Theological Seminary, Bonnie's real equipping for ministry came as she stepped into the role of primary caregiver, teacher and advocate for her daughter born with Down syndrome. Now, nineteen years after their daughter's birth, doors have opened for Bonnie and her husband to take the lessons learned and to reach out to families in their country of service with a message of hope.

**David C Deuel** is Senior Research Fellow (Policy and Publishing) for the Christian Institute on Disability and serves as Catalyst for Disability Concerns with the Lausanne Movement. Dave gained his MA from Cornell University, and MPhil and PhD from the University of Liverpool. He co-founded the North Los Angeles chapter of the National Down Syndrome Association. Dave has participated in disability outreach projects for children in eight countries. He was appointed Region Disability Integration Lead for the American Red Cross, and is a member of the United Nations Disability Data Working Group. He is founding editor for the *Journal for the Christian Institute on Disability.* Dave has served on the California State Council on Developmental Disabilities and currently participates in the New York State Developmental Disabilities Planning Council. He is married with four adult children; his youngest daughter has Down syndrome.

**Natalie Flickner** is an associate missionary with World Evangelism for Christ (WEC), serving as a part of Crisis Care Training International (CCTI). She graduated with degrees in both intercultural studies and Bible from Columbia International University. Then she continued studying at Columbia Biblical Seminary and earned an MA in pastoral counselling and spiritual formation. Natalie has ministered with CCTI since 2013. Her role at CCTI is Disability Coordinator and Trainer. Under this role, she has written a module for CCTI curriculum called 'Restoring Hope to Children with Disability.' She uses her personal experience of living with mild cerebral palsy in both her writing and speaking engagements.

**Barry Funnell**, although paraplegic due to an accident in 1982, qualified as a dentist in 1986. He and his wife, Julia, went to a mission training centre to study Bible translation. They then went to Malawi, where they trained a team of nationals to translate the Sena Bible in ten years. Barry obtained a MA in sociolinguistics, and went to Tanzania to start ten translation projects over five years. He now works as a Bible Translation consultant with The Word for the World. He travels from the UK to Africa and Southeast Asia, doing about eight international flights a year.

**Nathan G John** gained his doctorate at the University of Oxford. He is a Public Health Physician from Australia, and facilitates the CHGN Uttarakhand Cluster of fifty community health programs, which have a large disability focus. Nathan has worked in health and development in Africa, Fiji, East Timor, PNG, Bangladesh, Nepal and India. He researches on disability measurement and in 2011 he founded the Samvedna Community Based Disability program before working to establish a network of disability providers across India (Engage Disability). His firstborn daughter has a profound developmental disability, giving him a personal as well as professional interest in this area. For security reasons, given Nathan's involvement in a sensitive region of the world, his name has been changed.

**Paul Lindoewood** served as a Methodist Mission Partner based in Maua Hospital, Kenya, from 1996 to 2005. Rachel, Paul's wife, was a doctor there. Paul, who uses a wheelchair, has limited dexterity and communication impairments, was a Disability Community Worker. Paul and Rachel currently live in Brecon, South Wales, with their two children. Paul holds a bachelor's degree in public administration and a master's in disability studies. He has been active within the disability movement since the early eighties and currently is Coordinator of Disability in Wales and Africa, as well as being a trustee of the Brecon Molo Community Partnership.

**Jeff McNair** is professor of severe disabilities and disability studies at California Baptist University. He and his wife, Kathi, have led local church ministries to adults with disabilities since 1974. He has been involved in international training of leaders in areas of disability ministry and theology and has facilitated mission opportunities for persons with various disabilities.

**J M Paul** moved to South Asia with a bachelor's degree in nursing from Florida State University and a diploma in tropical nursing from the London School of Hygiene and Tropical Medicine. She is currently working part-time as an obstetrics nurse while she homeschools her children. She is passionate about women's health and maternal health care in rural South Asia. Since her time mothering Adam, she has become concerned and compelled towards those with disabilities in developing countries. You can find more of her writing at www.weunformed.com.

**Justin Reimer** and his wife, Tamara, are the proud parents of five children (Elisha, Noelle, Abram, Evangeline and Naomi). Elisha has Down syndrome. It was through their experience raising Elisha that The Elisha Foundation (TEF) was founded in 2005 as a means of outreach and care for families of children with special needs. The mission of TEF is the pursuit of Christ-centered transformation in the lives of those affected by disability through proclaiming biblical truth and providing needed resources. TEF provides family retreats and conferences, church training on disability and international outreach to special needs communities. The Reimer family currently lives and serves in Chernigov, Ukraine, working among the special needs community partnered locally with Christian Bible Church.

**Deanna Richey** has served in full-time Christian ministry with her family of six over the past twenty-five years in the USA and Australia. Having completed theological/counselling studies through Sydney College of Divinity in 2005, she earned an MA in member care in 2016 through Redcliffe/Gloucester. She now serves as the Director of Personnel and Member Care for SIM Australia, and balances this serving alongside her husband at Werribee Baptist Church, a thriving congregation made up of fifty-plus nationalities. Faced with many challenges throughout her own missionary journey, Deanna now passionately advocates for others seeking to follow God on mission.

# Notes

## Introduction

1. Quoted by Randy Alcorn, foreword to *Why, O God? Suffering and Disability in the Bible and Church*, ed. Larry J Waters and Roy B Zuck (Wheaton, IL: Crossway, 2011), 10.
2. www.engagedisability.com.
3. J E M Cameron, ed. *The Cape Town Commitment: A Confession of Faith and a Call to Action*, in *The Lausanne Legacy: Landmarks in Global Mission* (Lausanne Library/Hendrickson Publishers, 2016), 137.
4. 'Health Topics: Disabilities,' World Health Organization, accessed January 18, 2019, https://www.who.int/topics/disabilities/en/.
5. J Foxe, *Foxe's Book of Martyrs*, ed. Paul L Meier and R C Linnenkrugel (Grand Rapids: Kregel, 2016), 74.
6. *Wikipedia*, s.v. 'Lawrence of Rome,' last modified January 22, 2019, https://en.wikipedia.org/wiki/Lawrence_of_Rome.

## Chapter 1

1. Lynn Holden, *Forms of Deformity* (Sheffield: Sheffield Academic, 1991), 214; see the discussion of 1QSa 2.5–6 in D G Dunn, *The Acts of the Apostles* (Valley Forge, PA: Trinity Press International, 1996), 39–40.
2. Regarding the Old Testament term 'flesh' (*basar*), see Hans Walter Wolff, *Anthropology of the Old Testament* (Philadelphia: Fortress Press, 1974), 30–31. For a treatment of the Greek term 'flesh' (*sarx*) see David Alan Black, *Paul, Apostle of Weakness* (Eugene, OR: Pickwick Publications, 2012), 146.
3. Black, *Apostle of Weakness*, 154.
4. Black, *Apostle of Weakness*, 151.
5. See Jeremiah 15; Susan Niditch, *The Responsive Self: Personal Religion in Biblical Literature of the Neo-Babylonian and Persian Periods* (New Haven: Yale University Press, 2015), 64.
6. Moisés Silva, ed. *New International Dictionary of New Testament Theology and Exegesis*, s.v. '*asthenia*' (Grand Rapids: Zondervan, 2014), 4:316.
7. Lisa M Bowens, *An Apostle in Battle: Paul and Spiritual Warfare in 2 Corinthians 12:1–10* (Tübingen: Mohr Siebeck, 2017), 190–94. Bowens argues that Satan attacks Paul by sending a thorn and that the ongoing conflict with false apostles should be viewed collectively as a cosmic battle over which God triumphs.

8. Black, *Apostle of Weakness*, 161.
9. Black, *Apostle of Weakness*, 90.
10. Black, *Apostle of Weakness*, 81.
11. John K Chow, *Patronage and Power: A Study of Social Networks in Corinth* (Sheffield: Sheffield Academic, 1992), 178.
12. Ralph P Martin, *2 Corinthians* (Waco, TX: Word, 1986), 382.
13. Spoken by Dr. John MacArthur at Together for the Gospel conference, Twitter post by Richard Gregory, April 12, 2018, https://twitter.com/RichardPGregory/status/984504149978042369.

## Chapter 2

1. C L Seow, *A Grammar for Biblical Hebrew* (Nashville: Abingdon Press, 1995), 21.
2. William C Propp, *Exodus 1–18* (New York: Doubleday, 1998), 211.

## Chapter 3

1. Lon Solomon, *Brokenness: How God Redeems Pain and Suffering* (Potomac, MD: Red Door Press, 2005), 24.
2. Solomon, *Brokenness*, 14.
3. Solomon, *Brokenness*, 31.
4. Solomon, *Brokenness*, 40–41.
5. Solomon, *Brokenness*, 59–60.
6. Rick Langer, 'Disability, Calling and "A Kind of Life Imposed on Man,"' in *Beyond Suffering, Study Guide*, by Joni Eareckson Tada and Steve Bundy (Agoura Hills, CA: Joni and Friends, 2011).

## Chapter 5

1. C T Studd, *The Chocolate Soldier* (Fort Washington: CreateSpace Independent Publishing Platform, 2011).
2. O J Smith, *The Passion for Souls* (London: Marshall, Morgan and Scott, 1978).
3. Elisabeth Miller, *Operation Jonah* (Lake Mary, FL: Creation House, 2009).
4. William Carey, 'The Missionary Herald,' *The Baptist Magazine* 35 (1843): 41.

## Chapter 6

1. H Masters and W E Masters, *In Wild Rhodesia: A Story of Missionary Enterprise and Adventure in the Land Where Livingston Lived, Labored and Died* (London: Francis Griffiths, 1920), 199.

2. Olive Doke, 'Boreham and the Doke Connection,' *New Zealand Baptist*, January 1963, 4.
3. Olive Doke, *Paul the Leper, Apostle to the Lambas* (Johannesburg: South African Baptist Press, 1955; repr. 2005), 3.
4. Doke, *Paul the Leper*, 4.
5. Doke, *Paul the Leper*, 5.
6. Doke, *Paul the Leper*, 4.
7. Doke, *Paul the Leper*, 4.
8. Conrad Mbewe, *Insights from the Lives of Olive Doke and Paul Kasonga for Pioneer Mission and Church Planting Today* (Carlisle, UK: Langham Monographs, 2014), 106.
9. Mbewe, *Insights*, 7.
10. Mbewe, *Insights*, 11–12.
11. Doke, *Paul the Leper*, 10.
12. Doke, *Paul the Leper*, 13.
13. Doke, *Paul the Leper*, 13.
14. Mbewe, *Insights*, 112.
15. Mbewe, *Insights*, 112.
16. Holmes Rolston, *Personalities around Paul: Men and Women Who Helped or Hindered the Apostle Paul* (Richmond, VA: John Knox Press, 1955), 146.
17. Olive Doke, 'Report for the Year 1936,' *Lambaland Newsletter* 82 (1937): 1.
18. Mbewe, *Insights*, 177.
19. Doke, *Paul the Leper*, 10.
20. Mbewe, *Insights*, 173–74.
21. Mbewe, *Insights*, 120.
22. Doke, *Paul the Leper*, 1.
23. Personal interview of Elena Spider Cosamu with Conrad Mbewe in 2010, cited in Mbewe, *Insights*, 121.
24. Kevin Roy, preface to *Paul the Leper.*

## Chapter 7

1. '"Bad Legs"—Elinor, A Missionary Story.' YouTube video, 22:46, posted by Dianne Becker, June 15, 2015, https://www.youtube.com/watch?v=PuRvXePv_wA.

## Chapter 8

1. '7 Standards of Excellence,' The Standards of Excellence in Short-Term Mission, accessed January 24, 2019, https://soe.org/7-standards/.
2. R Peterson, *Maximum Impact Short-Term Mission: The God-Commanded Repetitive Deployment of Swift, Temporary Non-Professional Missionaries* (Orlando, FL: STEM Press, 2008), 19.

3. C Barnes, *'Cabbage Syndrome': The Social Construction of Dependency* (London: The Falmer Press, 1995), 9.
4. P Berger and T Luckman, *The Social Construction of Reality* (Garden City, NY: Doubleday, 1966), 1.
5. W Wolfensberger, *A Brief Introduction to Social Role Valorization: A High-Order Concept for Addressing the Plight of Societally Devalued People, and for Structuring Human Services*, 3rd ed. (Syracuse, NY: Training Institute for Human Service Planning, Leadership and Change Agentry, Syracuse University, 1998), 12–21.
6. D Wasserman, A Asch, J Blustein, and D Putnam, 'Disability: Definitions, Models, Experience,' in *The Stanford Encyclopedia of Philosophy*, Winter 2011, http://plato.stanford.edu/entries/disability/.
7. J McNair, 'Disability Studies Applied to Disability Ministry,' *Review and Expositor* 113.2 (2016): 159–66.

## Chapter 9

1. See Lausanne Occasional Paper 35B.
2. 'Children and Young People with Disabilities Fact Sheet,' UNICEF, May 2013, www.unicef.org/disabilities/files/Factsheet_A5__Web_REVISED.pdf.

## Chapter 11

1. N P Grubb, *C. T. Studd: Famous Athlete and Pioneer* (Grand Rapids: Zondervan, 1943).
2. C W Munyi, 'Past and Present Perceptions towards Disability: A Historical Perspective,' *Disability Studies Quarterly* 32.2 (2012), www.dsq-sds.org/article/view/3197/3068.
3. Australian Bureau of Statistics (ABS), 'National Survey of Mental Health and Wellbeing: Summary of Results,' 2015, accessed February 24, 2017, http://www.abs.gov.au/ausstats/abs@.nsf/mf/4430.0.
4. Munyi, 'Past and Present Perceptions.'
5. S Bryant and G Bryant, *Serving at the Ends of the Earth: Family Life and TCKs* (Coventry: WEC International, 2017).
6. D Lovell, *The Curious Incident of a Boy's Transformation: Helping a Child on the Autistic Spectrum* (Condeo Press, 2016).

## Conclusion

1. Solomon, *Brokenness*, 40–41.
2. C Spurgeon, *An All Round Ministry* (Charles River Editors, 2013), 384.

3. Australian Bureau of Statistics, 'National Survey.'
4. G Stott, *Twenty-Six Years of Missionary Work in China* (New York: American Tract Society, 1897), 2–3.
5. 'Health Topics: Disabilities,' World Health Organization, accessed January 18, 2019, https://www.who.int/topics/disabilities/en/.
6. K Donovan and R Myors, 'Reflections on Attrition in Career Missionaries: A Generational Perspective into the Future,' in *Too Valuable To Lose*, ed. William D Taylor (Pasadena, CA: William Carey Library, 1997), 41–69, http://www.worldevangelicals.org/resources/rfiles/res3_168_link_1292517737.pdf.
7. Please see Elinor Young's (World Team) endorsement at the beginning of this book. You can view her story '"Bad Legs"—Elinor, A Missionary Story' at www.youtube.com/watch?v=PuRvXePv_wA.

Connecting influencers and ideas for global mission

The Lausanne Movement takes its name from the International Congress on World Evangelization, convened in 1974 in Lausanne, Switzerland, by the US evangelist Billy Graham. His long-time friend John Stott, the UK pastor-theologian, was chief architect of *The Lausanne Covenant*, which issued from this gathering.

Two further global Congresses followed—the second in Manila, Philippines (1989) and the third in Cape Town, South Africa (2010). From the Third Lausanne Congress came *The Cape Town Commitment: A Confession of Faith and a Call to Action*. Its Call to Action was the fruit of a careful process conducted over four years to discern what we believe the Holy Spirit is saying to the global church in our times. In the words of the *Commitment*'s chief architect, Chris Wright, it expresses 'the conviction of a Movement and the voice of a multitude.'

The Lausanne Movement connects evangelical influencers across regions and across generations: in the church, in ministries and in the workplace. Under God, Lausanne events have often acted as a powerful catalyst; as a result, strategic ideas such as Unreached People Groups, the 10/40 Window, and holistic/integral mission have been introduced to missional thinking. Over 30 specialist Issue Networks now focus on the outworking of the priorities outlined in *The Cape Town Commitment*.

The movement makes available online over 40 years of missional content. Sign up to receive *Lausanne Global Analysis* to your inbox. Watch videos from Lausanne's gatherings. On the website you will also find a complete list of titles in the Lausanne Library.

**www.lausanne.org**

**Nearly 1 billion people around the world live with disabilities.**

For the past forty years, Joni and Friends' programs and outreaches around the world have presented the hope of the gospel to individuals and families of individuals affected by disability. We energize the church, moving people from lack of awareness to including everyone into the fabric of worship, fellowship, and outreach. We also train and mentor people with disabilities to exercise their gifts of leadership and service in their churches and communities.

**Joni and Friends' Mission**

To communicate the gospel and equip Christ-honoring churches worldwide to evangelize and disciple people affected by disabilities.

To learn more about Joni and Friends, please visit joniandfriends.org.